MW01096524

1

Mental Toughness & Iron Will:

Become Tenacious, Resilient, Psychologically Strong, and Tough as Nails

By Patrick King
Social Interaction Specialist and
Conversation Coach
www.PatrickKingConsulting.com

Table of Contents

Introduction

There are two passengers in the back of a taxi, and the taxi is in a minor car accident.

Neither passenger was hurt, and they both went home that night without a scratch on their heads. However, one passenger ruminated on the accident for weeks after, while the other nearly forgot about it when his coworker asked him how his week was.

What are the differences between these two people? You could say that one person was more sensitive to dangerous situations, or the other was more relaxed in their approach to life. These might be true, but ultimately, the major difference between these two people is their *mental toughness*. One person was able to process and move on, while the other remained stuck in their thoughts and headed down a dark road.

What is mental toughness, and why should you even care about it? It's not like you're dealing with potentially traumatic experiences on a daily basis. But every day, we make decisions that we know we shouldn't or that we feel too scared to refuse. For many of us, life is driven by fear, anxiety, and anticipation of the unknown. We're living to minimize mistakes and suffering as opposed to boldly seeking out exactly what we want.

Mental toughness is a trait that gets you out of this rut. It prepares you for the realities of the world and arms you with the means to achieve what you desire. A favorite quote of mine is "Life is tough, get a helmet"— that's exactly what mental toughness provides you with. Life with a helmet is life that is able to take risks and occasionally fail; life without a helmet is fearful and confined to a small comfort zone.

Mental toughness is about the will to carry on even when life is tough. It is the ability to bounce back and become stronger than before after failures. It means adjusting the voice inside your head to one that cheers you on and sneers at obstacles, instead of one who fixates on the worst-case scenario every single time.

Simply put, it's what separates people who are able to achieve what they want and those who end up with the lifelong habit of *settling*.

No one is born with a helmet, and that's what this book seeks to rectify.

Chapter 1. The Case of Mental Toughness

Steve works as a sixth-grade teacher at a large public middle school. He has been teaching for a number of years but has never been a standout employee. During his second year of teaching, he had a particularly difficult class and wasn't able to maintain order in his classroom. He often went home highly stressed and upset. He tried a few techniques for improving classroom management from his colleagues, but nothing seemed to make much difference. So he resigned himself to hoping for better-behaved students the next year.

He signed a contract to continue for a third year, but things only seemed to get worse. Was it the students, or was it him? Some of his classroom parents didn't approve of the reading materials he selected, he had a number of students with extremely low test scores, and his class was generally known as unruly and loud. Steve felt like more of a failure after every semester.

By year four, Steve was miserable. He felt beaten down and defeated. He didn't make much effort to improve his skills or try new methods to improve his classroom management. Shortly after winter break, Steve quit his job. Although he had massive student loans for six years of university courses to become a teacher, Steve decided to move out of the field of education.

Steve is not what we would consider mentally tough for a number of reasons. He left his future to chance by simply hoping for a better class each year instead of taking control of his situation and making changes to his teaching style, classroom management, or seeking additional support.

He didn't dust himself off after failures to try again; he would try a couple new techniques but quickly give up and hope his problems would simply go away. He wasn't able to apply any lessons that he had learned from prior failed school years to his present situation.

Ultimately, he decided to quit his job and move into an entirely different field, which precluded him from reaching his long-term career goals. Steve demonstrates how individuals that lack mental toughness may waste time, money, and sacrifice their chance at daily happiness. These individuals don't have the grit, drive, and stamina to change the things in their lives that can be changed and to learn from and embrace their failures to improve.

Why to Strive for Mental Toughness

Mental toughness is the ability to stay strong, even in the face of adversity. Life presents difficulties on a regular basis, just as it did for Steve. However, unlike Steve, those with mental toughness are able to keep their focus and determination. These people are able to learn from failures and be resilient in their thinking to overcome obstacles and challenges. They know what they want and have the means to get there *no matter what*. This ability to stay focused and learn from the past allows mentally tough people to achieve their long-term goals and overall success in life.

As we all know, events in our lives rarely go exactly as we plan them to, but letting small deviations and massive setbacks alike throw you off your game is a recipe for failure. Planning to avoid failure is a fool's errand; instead, plan for what happens when it inevitably comes.

Mental toughness allows you to learn from these difficulties, deviations, and even failure. Failure can be hard to overcome, mentally and emotionally, but those with mental toughness allow themselves time to process their feelings and simply move on. Mentally tough individuals know that to give up after failure simply leads to more failure. You have to learn from mistakes, get up, dust yourself off, and go at it again!

· This resilience and fortitude can give you the strength to keep your emotions under control when something seems overwhelming and you need to be strong. Essentially, mental toughness is that voice in the back of your head that tells you to keep going, to push through the difficulties, and to keep trying.

According to famed football coach Vince Lombardi, mental toughness is "a perfectly disciplined state of mind that refuses to give in." Mentally tough people don't just give up; they learn, adapt, and try again. The desire to give up because something seems that tough is all in your head; overcome your urges to take the easier option and quit. Discipline is required because it's no easy feat to refuse to take the easy road.

Researcher David Yukelson defines mental toughness as a *psychological edge that allows you to cope more effectively than your competition*. Yukelson goes on to say that mental toughness is the ability to perform consistently better than your competition.

At work, in the gym, and even in our families we want to be the best that we can be, and usually that means being better than the person next to you on the Stairmaster. The world does not work in a vacuum, and we are only mentally tough relative to who else is competing for our same goals. Employing and honing your mental toughness can give you the little extra boost that you need to be the best version of yourself, whether that is doing the tenth rep at the gym when your partner only does nine, negotiating the highest possible salary rate for your new position at work, or helping your child with her math homework more effectively than the parents of other children in her class.

However, your competition doesn't always have to be another person; sometimes, your competition can just be the part inside of you that wants to quit or take an easier route. Employing your mental toughness to beat out that little negative voice in your head is just as important as running a faster mile than your old high school gym buddy.

It could be argued that most of us probably don't have the necessary mental toughness to push through life's greatest challenges. Many of us are emotionally fragile and take challenging events to heart; you might even be someone who struggles when faced with overwhelming odds.

This is likely true—for the time being, at least. It's a temporary condition that will shortly be rectified.

You probably want to become more resilient, more resolute, and more mentally tough when facing life's difficulties. But is that even possible? Are some people simply born mentally tough, while others have to struggle through life? Could Steve have made different choices that would have guided him to have success with his future classes? Was Steve destined to quit a career he had worked so hard and long for? Of course not.

Mental toughness *isn't* something people are born with. Just like some of us happen to be better at baseball than others, it is similarly a skill that can be developed over time. Mental toughness comes through experience, through learning from failures, and through the decisions we make when handling difficult circumstances in our lives. Steve could have learned to adapt through handling his failures in a positive manner and learning from his experiences.

Recall the advice from the introduction, "When life gets tough, get a helmet." The tactics presented in this book can help you to create the helmet that you need to achieve mental toughness.

It's not what happens to us in life that matters; it's how we perceive and react to these events that earns us the badge of mental toughness. Mental toughness is all about choice. It's about the decisions you make in the moment and the habits you establish over time.

Are you choosing to give up, or are you embracing mistakes as the opportunities that they are to learn and overcome the same situations if you encounter them in the future? Are you quick to anger or anxiety when faced with unexpected changes, or do you remain calm and commit to decisions only after you have logically thought through your options? These types of choices distinguish mentally tough individuals from the rest of the pack. You've got no choice at what happens *to* you, but everything else is up to you.

Your brain is constantly establishing and reinforcing habits over time, and the majority of this habit formation happens unconsciously. Those with mental toughness know how to harness the power of habit formation to reverse negative habits and cultivate resiliency. This type of thinking and these positive habits are some of the skills that will be discussed in this book. Concrete and approachable methods will be listed so that no matter where you are in your journey toward mental toughness, you will have new ideas and processes to take away and apply to your life immediately.

We all know you can't control many things that happen during the course of your life, but you can control how you respond to these events. No matter how prepared you are or how hard you try, sometimes you simply won't get the raise you ask for or the promotion you feel you deserve.

For many people, this is enough to cause them to give up. But mentally tough people know that to give up means there will be no future chances for promotion or a raise. Choosing to persevere in these types of situations is the only way to overcome them. This theme will repeat throughout your life, and the more times you are able to make the choice to persevere through hardship and come out successful on the other side, the greater confidence you will have in your ability to overcome anything that life can throw at you. When you feel mentally strong, you can rise up to meet any obstacle that life presents.

The Biology and Physiology of Mental Toughness

Building mental toughness isn't only about making choices; there are also biological and physiological components. Taking the time to understand how your body is programmed to react in stressful situations allows you to step back and view your feelings and emotions through a scientific, logical lens. This can help keep you from making hasty, emotional decisions and also allows you to capitalize on the processes your body is going through anyway to increase your mental toughness.

John Coates, president of the Australian Olympic Committee, makes the argument that, similar to building a world-class athlete, mental toughness depends on your ability to constantly switch between anabolic and catabolic states. When you're in a catabolic state, you're in a state of stress, and when you're in an anabolic state, you're in a state of rest. Thus, mental toughness depends on training our minds to navigate the balance between being

21

stressed and resting. At first glance, this is logical because if we can't escape our stressed moods, then we will eventually break down.

For instance, athletes know that a common method used in training to run faster is spending short periods of time sprinting at top speed and alternating this with periods of walking. This interval training makes you faster and increases how long you can run without exhaustion. To increase mental toughness, you can use the same idea: short periods of stress alternated with periods of rest. Let's look at the biology behind this.

Viewing mental toughness from a biological and physiological standpoint, there are three distinct chemical classes that control mental toughness and this process of alternating between stress and rest: catabolic hormones, anabolic hormones, and amines.

The Stress Reaction. As mentioned, the stress reaction is controlled by catabolic hormones. Cortisol is a chemical that is released when we are stressed. It is a vital part of supplying the human body with energy during periods of extreme mental or physical effort. Of course, this is paired with adrenaline and known as the fight-or-flight instinct. Cortisol's job is to increase our performance potential and allow our brains to get in "the zone" during urgent periods.

The downside is that in order to supply this immediate energy, cortisol strips our body of nutrients. If our body continues to use cortisol for days or weeks on end, we begin to experience a lack of nutrition. Those who suffer from long-term stress tend to have chronic mental and physical ailments, which are partially due to the constant use of cortisol. For maximum efficiency, cortisol should only be used by the brain in short bursts. This is typically the state people need to cope with to become mentally tough.

The Repair Reaction. The rest, or repair, reaction is controlled by anabolic hormones. These hormones repair the damage done to the body by the catabolic hormones. During this rest period, anabolic hormones work to return the body to its baseline state.

Insulin and insulin-like growth factor (IGF) are also anabolic hormones. IGF's job is to rejuvenate cells, including brain cells. Ideally, the number of anabolic hormones in your body should be larger than the number of catabolic hormones. This ratio is called the growth index. The higher the growth index, the greater the individual's capacity to rebuild their body after a stressful period. The essence of this ratio is the amount of cortisol present in a body in comparison to the amount of testosterone. Individuals must maintain some cortisol, but we need a higher level of testosterone to overcome mental and physical obstacles successfully.

Amines. The anabolic and catabolic states *can* flow directly into the other, but that is a much slower process, which correlates to lower mental toughness. When you're in an anabolic resting state, there are actually two pathways your brain can take to deal with a stressor.

This alternative step is triggered by *amines*. Amine chemicals switch on and off quickly. Interestingly enough, the strength of an amine response is an accurate way to determine an individual's level of mental toughness. A stronger amine response indicates a faster hormonal switch to rest and repair from the harmful stress and anxiety phase.

Amines focus our attention, increase our ability to concentrate, and promote the fight-or-flight response. Amines serve a nearly identical purpose to catabolic hormones; however, because they are present in the bloodstream for such a short period of time, they are not as damaging to the body.

In tough individuals, amine levels rise more quickly and prominently when stressed or threatened and then shut off quickly as soon as the immediate threat is disposed of. And because this individual is able to handle stress more aptly, the body's equilibrium is not thrown off balance and there is no long-lasting emotional distress.

Along with the interplay between stressed and restful states, the concept of ego depletion also figures into one's amount of mental toughness. You might experience this most tangibly in the context of making decisions or exercising willpower.

Ego depletion is the idea that our mental resources for specific activities are limited. When the resources drain or are decreased, those specific mental activities perform poorly. It was first discovered in relation to self-control, where experiments (Roy Baumeister, 1998) showed that subjects who resisted chocolate performed worse and gave up earlier on a puzzle task. In other words, ego depletion was in full effect, and the amount of self-control they exhibited in resisting the chocolate directly weakened their ability to persist with the puzzle task. Decision quality decreased quickly as ego depletion started to take place.

Imagine having a bucket filled with mental toughness. Every time we force ourselves to do something we'd rather not, we dip into the bucket. Every time we are stressed or anxious and keep it together, we dip into the bucket. As we go through our days, the bucket naturally empties from fatigue, hunger, and general wear and tear.

The brain requires energy to act and think. In fact, the brain requires up to 20% of our daily energy consumption, despite being only 2% of the mass of our bodies. It works hard, and the act of self-control is not something that's easy.

It's easy to resist chocolate once or twice, but when you encounter the temptation repeatedly throughout the day, your self-control will likely erode, and it will become nearly impossible to say no—because your brain will run out of juice to do so. The same goes for mental toughness and making decisions that go against what you *really* want to do.

No matter how resilient or persevering you might be, it's impossible to not falter after a certain point. Ego depletion is a real factor in just how mentally tough we can be at any given moment.

Mental Toughness Mantra

To cap off our introduction into mental toughness, it's helpful to keep a few things in mind right from the start. We can call this our mental toughness mantra, which sets up how we want to think differently and what we want to accomplish. If nothing else, think of it as an inspirational way to cap off the first chapter before moving into more detailed discussion of how to be resilient and tough.

I believe and I know:

Adversity is a temporary condition.

Adversity does more good than bad.

Failure is feedback.

Failure has purpose, and it may not always be immediate.

Persistence will always make the difference.

Persistence is just around the corner.

Takeaways:

- Mental toughness is more than a trait; it's a way of looking at life. Life is tough, so you better get a helmet. Point being, adversity and failure aren't things to plan around—that is impossible. What we should be doing is planning for them and thinking to the next step of how we will react and get back up. That is mental toughness at its core.
- Surprisingly, mental toughness has biological components to it. This manifests mostly in two ways. First, there is an interplay with stressed and rest states, mediated by how strong our amine response is. The stronger the amine response, the less we stress and grow anxious. Second, the concept of ego depletion applies handily to mental

toughness. Generally this means that our willpower and discipline wears down with mental fatigue, and it applies to toughness as well. Thankfully, this is something you can plan around if you are aware of it.

- What kind of mantra should you repeat to yourself regarding toughness? It involves adversity, failure, and persistence. Adversity is good, failure is inevitable, and persistence is the secret sauce.

Chapter 2. Facing Failure and Fear

Casey was feeling down on her luck. She'd been applying for jobs but had only gotten a few interviews. At first, she took it in stride. Lots of people face challenges when they're job-hunting, she told herself. Not everyone gets a job right away, and it's unreasonable to expect instant success in any walk of life.

As the days stretched into weeks, she started thinking that maybe *she* was the problem. This is my fault, she thought. Unconsciously, she started keeping a list of all the reasons she was undesirable as an employee. When she would apply for new jobs or write cover letters, her heart wasn't in it as she never quite thought she would have a chance. She was taking herself out of the game without realizing it.

One day Casey found herself grousing internally about her bad luck, and all of a sudden, as if she'd heard a voice actually say it, she thought, *ENOUGH*. She realized that her attitude was affecting her job search. If she faltered now, when she was up against a few minor setbacks, then what would happen when she got a job and faced real challenges?

She remembered a class she took in college about Buddhist beliefs and how Buddhists are trained to believe in impermanence of both happiness and sadness. If everything was fleeting, then what's bad shall pass soon enough, she reasoned to herself. If life was a series of ebbs and flows, then her luck would eventually change. All she had to do was do her best to believe in herself and know that both happiness and sadness were impermanent states—she just happened to be in a negative state that would pass shortly.

So she reconsidered the way she'd been approaching her hunt for a job. She rewrote her resume and began reading employment blogs to pick up interviewing tips. She decided to look at rejection as a way to learn and adapt for those inevitable happy periods, which would also be impermanent. Soon enough, calls for interviews turned into job offers.

Many people will find themselves in situations like Casey's at some point in their lives. They encounter a setback or an obstacle in their process and then they don't know what to do next. Indeed, we are never taught a roadmap to deal with rejection and failure or even the prospect of those crippling psychological forces. Casey was lucky that she was able to grasp on to some age-old wisdom from Buddhism, which is something we'll cover shortly in this chapter.

But what other ways can we equip ourselves to deal with failure and fear? This might be one of the cornerstone questions of what makes one person mentally tough and another not—the ability to deal with life as it comes, for better or worse.

No one will ever talk about needing mental toughness when everything is smooth sailing, so what happens when you hit an iceberg and have to scramble? It's a waste of time to plan to avoid those icebergs—if you avoid the first layer of icebergs, you'll just get nailed at the second or third layer. Therefore, we should prepare for what happens in those inevitable moments of pain. Those are the moments that define your character, and that's what this chapter is about.

There are a few different ways people can cope with tough periods in their lives. One way, for example, is by taking a Buddhist approach. It's worth consideration even if you're not a practicing Buddhist.

Buddhist Philosophies

It helps to know a little about the beginning of Buddhism and where it came from. The

Buddha is not a deity in the traditional sense, and he is not to be worshipped as other religions worship a central figure. Buddha began life as a prince known as Siddhartha Gautama. He traveled widely in his princely duties and began to wonder if there was a way to alleviate or even to avoid the suffering he saw so common in his lands. He was deeply troubled by the fact that, no matter how powerful you were, nobody could escape the pains caused by illness, aging, and death.

So he set off on a quest for wisdom and eventually came to the realization that suffering could be stopped, so he began to enlighten others to the methods he saw to stop personal and societal suffering. Gradually, he was bestowed the title of Buddha, which means "the awakened one."

His general teachings were that the cause of suffering was right in front of our faces, and we possessed the power to be just as happy as we wanted to be. How can this be?

Buddhism makes the assumption that suffering is a result of our desires and expectations, rather than our realities. In other words, what doesn't exist, and may never exist, is what is actually making us suffer. It's quite illuminating to realize that you may have rooted your hopes and dreams in the future or past, with little regard to the present moment and how you feel *right now*. Indeed, you are solely responsible for how fulfilled and happy you feel.

Accept this moment as it is. Thus, one of Buddhism's greatest tenets is to accept the status quo for what it is, whatever it is. A person who has hit a rough patch must accept it and not try to rush past it or ignore it. You don't have to like it, but you must understand that it's where you are now. You can't fast-forward or rewind your life. Trying to resist the moment will only compound your suffering. The important thing to remember is that this moment won't last. Everything is temporary, for better or worse.

Every moment, even a bad one, ends. So while you may be struggling this moment or even the next, your struggles *will* come to an end. Accepting the moment will help your struggle end more quickly. Once you can understand this, you can relax into the present.

You may balk at this because you want your life to change immediately. It's okay to want change. In fact, it's essential to life, because a seed that doesn't change never sprouts and grows into a tree. But it is under no obligation to change and grow at your desired pace.

Accept a negative reality such as a car accident, because once you have acceptance, you can plan how to move forward. Don't compare your moment to your pre-car accident past and the expectations you had for the future of where you wanted to drive. Those don't exist anymore and shouldn't influence how you feel about the current moment, which is its own independent entity.

Accept that life can never be perfect. Nothing in life is perfect. This is the second lesson you can learn from Buddhist thought. The faster you release expectations of perfection, the faster you can end your struggling. It's an unrealistic expectation, and one that makes you hate anything that falls short of it. You're setting yourself up for failure when you have the slightest inclination toward perfection. When would you ever be able to find contentment?

Furthermore, the second you feel it might be perfect, it will be gone in a flash. You will look toward the future, toward that one thing—a new job, a new car, a new home— that you're convinced will bring happiness. It doesn't matter whether you get that shiny new thing or not; new expectations are just around the corner to always keep you dissatisfied.

You may think that you'll be happy once some future event occurs, but what usually happens is that you then find a new future event upon which to stake your future bliss. Depending on *something* to make you happy is actually what is preventing your happiness. If you can learn to let go of those expectations that happiness is rooted in certain events, belongings, possessions, or status, then what is happiness based on?

We have to let go of our ideas about how life must turn out before we can finally be happy.

Suffering shows you a path. Who wants to embrace struggling or suffering? However, this line of thought isn't all about suffering. According to Buddhist thought, suffering is inevitable, roughly 50% of life by the law of averages. So what do we do? Turn away and run from 50% of the events in our lives?

No. Buddhism may sound masochistic, but the truth is that it simply places the power in your hands. Just as you delight in your successes and happiness, you should pay a similar amount (not type) of attention to your suffering and unhappiness. This allows you to *change* it; your suffering has shown you a direct path toward enlightenment.

You can do this by taking a clear-eyed assessment of the situation in which you find yourself. You're not meant to wallow in your misery but instead to analyze and face what's going on.

So instead of choosing coping mechanisms that can be unhealthy, like eating your feelings or drowning them in alcohol, you can use this time to better yourself. You could ask yourself, for example, what you can learn from this experience. If you take the time to do that now, then you arm your future self with the tools to weather storms with grace. Maybe this part of your life isn't about escaping but about preparing.

You might be thinking that this sounds like difficult work, especially when you're afraid or angry. Stressful situations can have physical effects, making you feel like you can't breathe without screaming. If this is the case for you, then you can use another lesson from Buddhism and use mindfulness. Mindfulness gives you breathing room, sometimes literally, if you need it.

A common way is simply to breathe deeply, in and out. Then focus on your breathing, with four seconds inhaling followed by four seconds exhaling. That's all there is to it. When your thoughts drift, bring them back to your breathing. It allows you that moment to notice what you're thinking and feeling without becoming consumed by your emotions. Just as with anything you practice, the more you do it, the easier it will become.

So while hard times are unavoidable, according to Buddhism you should face those moments. If this seems challenging, remember that you do it for others. When you see someone in distress, you acknowledge that they're hurting and then you try to comfort them. This rolls directly into the next Buddhist tenet.

Be kind to yourself and others. What does this mean, exactly? When a friend is being self-critical, you don't join in. You assure them their fears are unfounded and you might even argue with them not to talk that way about your friend. Show yourself the same compassion. In fact, you wouldn't dare talk to a friend the way you talk to yourself.

Could you be the very cause of your own suffering from a lack of self-empathy and self-compassion?

This is important because Buddhists believe that mindfulness can't exist without compassion. Think of the weight we place on a doctor's bedside manner. A physician may be skilled, but they can make a tough situation a lot less stressful just by their attitude. The way you deal with yourself and others can be a net positive or net negative. However, you don't have to be a doctor to benefit from using kindness.

You may, for example, know someone who prides himself on his honesty. That might even be you. However, without kindness, stark honesty can come across as harsh. It can also wear you down emotionally after a while. It's much easier to be kind, no matter the message.

If kindness doesn't come naturally to you, it's like anything else. You can work at it. Just as with suffering, if you spend too much time indulging in negative feelings, like cynicism and criticism, you can find yourself overwhelmed. They become easy and kindness may feel strange.

It's vital for your development and resilience that you start practicing. The easiest way to start practicing kindness with yourself is to start practicing it with other people. In being kind to others, it's easier to be kind to yourself. It then becomes a self-fulfilling prophecy, like a circle of kindness, in which your kindness to yourself feeds your kindness to others and then back again. This circle of kindness can then give you the strength to move forward through the rough patches.

Being kind to yourself means accepting flaws and moving through life while giving yourself the benefit of the doubt. Self-love can help you confront the painful aspects of your life, which will then help you recognize the pain of others. It's important then to remember that this is not weakness. Instead, what builds our courage and our resilience in the face of struggle.

Struggle and suffering are inevitable, but they are only a series of moments— moments that are destined to eventually pass. Then you will find yourself in a new moment, one that's ripe with possibilities. Every day, you have the opportunity to move forward and to find happiness. It all depends on how you respond to each moment.

This means that you can alter your way of thinking and tend toward happiness, even in the face of what you fear the most. Remember that Buddhism centers around the idea of impermanence, so whatever obstacle you face is destined to fade away eventually. You might be able to influence the rate at which it fades, but even if you do not, things will be all right in the end. So while there is suffering in the world, and you won't be able to avoid it, you can choose how you react. The power to end your suffering is truly within your hands alone; relying on anything or anyone else is a dangerous game.

Learning from Failure

As has been made clear, failure and fear are not things you can plan to avoid. You can plan around them, but not plan to avoid them. The ship you're steering will inevitably hit an iceberg, but that iceberg doesn't necessarily have to sink you. What you do after you're hit will determine that; how you choose to respond is at the crux of handling setbacks. You can harness your setback into a learning experience, though admittedly it will never be our first instinct.

There are several common ways that people react when they're faced with resistance. Usually, these ways are rooted in emotion—they are emotional responses. We know that, by definition, emotional responses don't often overlap with a reasoned and rational response. They are intense and reactive to the point of being detrimental, but it cannot be helped, for such is human nature.

For instance, one common emotional response to resistance is to blame himself or herself.

It's okay to be critical, even self-critical, as this is the engine of growth and development. But you can also take it too far. When you blame your issues on yourself in a way that assumes that any problems you have are based on a permanent flaw, then you don't allow yourself room for growth. You also don't give yourself the ability to rebound. All you do is put yourself in a situation where you can never win and were destined to be the villain. Blaming yourself might be a stage you must pass through, so all you can hope to do most of the time is to keep this stage quick.

Another way to respond to hardship is by simply not responding.

You might just pretend that your struggle isn't happening. You can call this denial, pretending nothing is afoot, or pretending that it doesn't warrant your attention. Whatever the case, you don't deal with it— dealing with it might force you to confront some ugly truths that you'd rather sweep under the carpet. However, while this is an easy path to take, it's not one you can take repeatedly and for an extended period of time. Things will catch up to you eventually, and you will suffer from your prolonged lack of response. The so-called ostrich method of plunging your head into the sand will seldom work.

Instead of the prior two methods of response, you could react to failure or a setback in a way that can help you grow. That way is by trying to understand the experience. This can be a painful process, because it may force you to confront things about you or your history that are unpleasant. However, this is the only way out of the three that you can use to transform your world.

If you choose one of the first two ways, either being hard on yourself or avoiding the problem, then it's easier to pretend that your struggle is happening in a vacuum. You're just having a temporary issue and some external factor is to blame. For example, maybe you got a poor performance review at work. While it would be easy to blame the bad review on an overly stringent boss or to ignore the review completely, in the long run it won't help you.

However, if you were to look closer at yourself and your work, you would likely find room for improvement. Finding the true cause is a large component of understanding the failure. Maybe your work *has* been sloppy, and you'll find that when you're honest with yourself, it's not up to your standards, either. Maybe it'll turn out that the work just isn't for you and you're meant to be somewhere else or to do something else. You won't find this out if you don't face it.

This is easier to talk about than do. Many of us are not wired that way. Instead, we have gotten used to reacting emotionally. Failure is emotional. It hurts. Our lizard brains take over, and they are not known for their rationality or self-awareness. So you'll instinctually walk down the path of dreaming up worst-case scenarios until you can think clearly again. By that point, it might be too late.

We do this not only because it's instinctual, but also because it protects us from being hurt. However, we will only stay in this cycle of hurt if we don't do anything to move beyond it.

You might remember, for instance, learning to ride a bike. At some point, unless you were a bike-riding prodigy, you probably fell. If you still went on to learn to ride, it's because you got back on the bike. Further, to learn to ride, you had to get on the bike in the first place. It's the same with overcoming fear and failure.

You can't overcome failure without acting. Yes, you tried something and you failed. Unless you've been unusually lucky, it wasn't the first time and it won't be the last time that you fail at something. However, you tried and you can try again. Failure is not the end.

If you polled any and all people you might consider successful, they'd tell you that their success came after multiple failures. They may not even realize it because they pivoted so quickly after a series of red flags, but never was their ascent linear like a straight line. It always involved zigs and zags that represented having to change gears and adapt.

What separates successful people from people who can't seem to overcome their failures is that successful people use failure as a learning experience. It's not enough to move through a failure. You must examine it and use it as an opportunity to prepare yourself for the future, which will include future failures.

One of the most effective ways to learn from failure is to question the failure. While it's true that some obstacles in your life may seem insurmountable, they only seem this way if you're not trying all you can think of to scale them. You can do this by asking the right questions. These include questions concerning what you can learn from the experience and typically end in concrete solutions and answers about how to act differently.

How can I do this better? Are your methods fatally flawed and crumble under greater scrutiny? Are you missing a crucial element that would make things easier and more efficient?

What can I learn from this experience? What did you learn that works? Do you understand what made the difference? Where was the flaw and what else needs to be fixed?

How can I make the most of my predicament? What did you learn not to do, and how will you do it differently next time? What's the next best step to do in light of the predicament, and what ways can it be salvaged?

What can I do here that I hadn't considered before? What did you miss and need to spend time exploring? What assumptions were wrong and need to be re-evaluated?

It's like learning to swim the backstroke. It is composed of many parts, and at first, you might swallow a few mouthfuls of water trying to learn it. But eventually, you will learn to keep your head above the water line. Then you will learn how your legs and arms can move in sync with each other. Then you might be able to learn how to do kick turns when you reach ends of the pool.

But you will never learn those things unless you stop, analyze what you did wrong, and learn from your failures. However, if you challenge yourself to learn one thing from each of your failed attempts, then you will be better-equipped when you encounter the next failure. You can move on from setbacks, but the only way to do that is to start moving and learning.

Setbacks are unavoidable, but like Casey and her job interviews, you can find a way to move past them. Even if you encounter failures, you can figure out how to turn them into successes. Those situations might not turn out like you'd hoped, but if you look at them with the right eyes, you can use them to shape the way you react and respond in the future. Your mental toughness is just like your physical toughness—you have to exercise to make it stronger.

Amor Fati

In order to move past some common fears about the situations life can bring, German philosopher Friedrich Nietzsche provides some insight on how to be satisfied with what life dishes out.

> *"My formula for what is great in mankind is amor fati: not to wish for anything other than that which is; whether behind, ahead, or for all eternity. Not just to put up with the inevitable—much less to hide it from oneself, for all idealism is lying to*

oneself in the face of the necessary—
but to love it."

Amor fati, which means literally the love of fate, simply means to accept and love everything that happens. In other words, Nietzsche offers the key to a happy life: do not wish for reality to be any different; rather, accept and love whatever happens. The parallels to Buddhism should be clear.

Some things are going to happen that will create a fear response. There is no way around it. Nietzsche's advice is to simply accept the situation as it is—no wishing it away or agonizing over it. When you agonize over something, you are causing yourself to suffer twice—with the ruminating beforehand and the actual event, if it even occurs.

Consider the ancient metaphor of being leashed to a cart: the wise man is like a dog leashed to a moving cart, running joyfully alongside and smoothly keeping pace with it; the foolish man is like a dog that struggles against the leash but finds himself dragged beside the cart anyway. Both dogs are in the same situation, but which one has the better journey and feels less resistance and more happiness? Obviously, it is the one who does not fight what he cannot beat.

We have the option of going along and enjoying the ride, or we have the option of fighting and complaining all the way. Since nobody wants to be dragged along, the best thing we can do is make the most of the journey and plan for the journey itself rather than fuss about how bad it might be. Nietzsche would advise us to embrace fear, even when it is paralyzing—because what else is there to do from a fatalistic standpoint?

Complaining will not help, and pulling away will not help, but moving forward and facing what comes allows us to experience all sorts of terrain: joy, love, excitement, boredom, sadness, and, yes, even fear. The key is to keep going forward, along for the ride, no matter what we face.

Does this sound like you are simply caving to fear? Just because people try to love what happens does not mean they condone or approve of it. It simply means they understand they cannot change it, so the best option is to accept it and try to make the best of it. Then people can identify the best action to take in the situation— something wholly missing if you choose to focus on how bad it will be. By embracing fate, we embrace our failures, our success, our powerlessness—all of those things we find terrifying and immobilizing.

The idea is simple: take every moment as it is; take reality as it is; do not resist or it will have power over you; if you take it as it comes, it will have no power over you. It is a simple idea but difficult to put into practice. One way to put this philosophy into action is by recognizing that things come and go.

Vernon Howard offers the following: "We can see that our pain lies between what we think should happen and what actually happens. Then, if we remove the secret demand for this or that to happen, the pain-gap vanishes."

The concept of amor fati, accepting and loving whatever fate brings to life, allows people to develop a life philosophy that almost laughs in the face of fear. Instead of being afraid of the unknown, embrace it. Instead of fearing failure, accept it. Instead of worrying about the judgment of others, let it roll off without giving it any consideration at all.

The question still remains, however: how does a person love fate when fate sometimes brings negative things? For example, when fate brings a job loss, how can that be something to love? Or when fate results in a relationship ending, how can that be something to love?

Loving fate does not mean celebrating when something horrible happens but shifting your mindset to look past it and adapt.

Consider the loss of a job. It is one of those situations that people fear will happen, and then they are filled with fear when it does happen. It makes people feel inferior to others. Additionally, there are serious and fear-inducing consequences of a job loss. On all fronts, it is a horrible situation.

By embracing amor fati, you would accept the loss and move on to whatever fate brings. Perhaps it becomes a chance to explore a new job focus; perhaps it is a catalyst for starting that small business that, up until now, was only a daydream; perhaps it is the motivation to return for additional training or education.

In any case, there is no way to move backward or even stay stagnant, so your only choice is to embrace the present and move forward. Love the possibilities that are now presented to you and the various types of futures that are now able to exist. Just as fate takes away, it can provide in the very next moment.

Sound scary? It probably will be. Your fears are what will prevent you from living this way, if you let them. Instead of allowing fear to dictate your attitude toward fate, fearlessly take fate as it comes.

Takeaways:

- Can you plan your life to avoid fear and failure? Yes, but that would lead to a life of emptiness. To achieve any measure of happiness and success in life, elements of fear and failure will always be present. Not everything will always go your way. So instead of planning to avoid failure, plan for what happens when you inevitably sail into an iceberg. You may be able to steer clear of the first one, but the second or third will get you eventually.
- Buddhist philosophy is a helpful lens to look at failure through. What is failure to Buddhists? Unpleasant, but impermanent and necessary. Life goes through ebbs and flows, and the only constant is change. Accepting this will help negative moments pass more easily, as will accepting that perfection is impossible. Moreover, our suffering shows us a path to greater fulfillment

and happiness. Buddhism is about understanding that your life is like a wave that gives and takes equally.

- Fear and failure are your ultimate teachers. When you fail, typical responses include blaming yourself or denial. These are instinctual because failure is an emotional event, and our lizard brains rush to protect ourselves. But failure is best when you can look at it and give it equal time as your successes. This allows you to understand and deconstruct how to never fail in that context again. Your very worst-case scenario is not failing; it is being able to learn from it.

- *Amor fati* literally means to love fate. Does that mean you should love whatever obstacles or failures you come across? Of course, not. But you can love the infinite possibilities and futures you now have access to. Acceptance, similarly to Buddhism, is important, because to struggle with or deny failure is to cause oneself unnecessary pain.

Chapter 3. Mind Over Heart

Having control over your emotions is an important aspect that characterizes mental toughness. Having control over your emotions does not simply mean suppressing them. Mentally tough individuals still experience their emotions; however, they do not let their emotions dictate their decision-making.

Part of the reason mental toughness is difficult to achieve is due to the necessity of keeping our emotions in check. Emotions hijack our mental processes and leave us agonizing over a decision or cause us to make a terrible choice, even when logically it is very clear what choice should be made.

People who are not in control of their emotions react with anger or sadness when something doesn't go as planned. This behavior can be alienating to spouses, children, coworkers, and friends. Mentally tough people refuse to let outside circumstances affect their plans. Regardless of what difficult situations life may throw at them, these individuals keep their emotions in check and continue moving toward their long-term goals.

To achieve mental toughness, being aware of and in control of your emotions is paramount. Out-of-control thoughts and feelings lead to reactive, nonlogical decisions; fragile states where you can become paralyzed with indecision; or easily excitable mindsets in which many poor and contradictory decisions are made. Working toward mental toughness helps you avoid all of this and instead allows you to make calm, cool decisions that help you make strides forward toward the life you want to lead.

Expressing Your Emotions

Sandra's mother was recently diagnosed with dementia. She is an only child, so all of the required caretaking quickly fell to her. Between taking her mother to doctor's appointments, preparing food, and completing the daily tasks required at two homes—Sandra was exhausted.

Sandra had always been described as a perfectionist, so although she felt overwhelmed, she suppressed her emotions and carried on with her duties. By rushing from doctor's appointment to doctor's appointment, she was able to completely bottle her feelings and act as though nothing major had occurred in her life.

A few weeks went by and Sandra began to feel run down. Although she was exhausted, she found it difficult to fall asleep at night due to anxiety about her mother's condition. She often found herself snapping at her husband and daughter. At work, she began to forget deadlines and even forgot a few important details regarding a client's file.

Finally, at one of her mother's doctor's appointments, the physician mentioned that Sandra looked stressed. The physician advised Sandra to acknowledge her feelings and spoke about the stress relief that can often be found through journaling or giving oneself time to cry.

Although it felt foreign, Sandra decided to give herself some space to write about her feelings. Over the course of a week she noticed a significant difference in her concentration, work performance, and patience with her family. It almost felt like magic how quickly she noticed herself bouncing back to her normal equilibrium.

As you can see, suppressing your emotions is not healthy or effective. Mentally tough individuals express and experience their emotions but ensure that they do so in a way that is not detrimental. That's the major difference. By expressing and experiencing your emotions you are able to think clearly and calmly and move forward to deal with whatever obstacle you are facing. Sandra was able to capitalize on journaling as a form of emotional expression to help her release her feelings and avoid the stress that comes from ignoring one's emotions.

A surprising series of studies on crying by the American Psychological Association (APA) revealed evidence on the importance of not suppressing emotions. The APA found that most people feel relieved after crying due to stress from interpersonal relationships or anxious, sad thoughts. A 1983 study showed that crying is one of the most effective ways to filter out the negative thoughts that cause worry. Suppressing your emotions, whether anger, sadness, or fear, can lead to long-term psychological damage.

Crying releases negative tension that builds up from the everyday occurrences in our lives. Emotional tears contain hormones that escape our body, which ultimately improves our mood after crying. It was determined by a biochemist that emotional tears contain more protein than nonemotional tears, such as those released from chopping an onion. This is an indication that important psychological and physiological changes happen within the body during the emotional release of crying. After crying, people often feel recharged, comforted, and filled with the energy to pick themselves up and continue moving forward.

Deep, emotional crying involves very specific physical processes including muscular spasms, rapid breathing, and tears. These symptoms quickly increase, come to a climax, and then gradually subside. Throughout this process, the body goes through a series of tensing and relaxing motions, which provides a feeling of release. This causes the dissipation of stress and the related psychological symptoms.

Allowing yourself the time and space to cry acts as a powerful catharsis and lets you move forward with your tension released. During stressful situations, stepping back and taking the time to feel your emotions sets you up to think logically about solutions or next steps without having anxiety or depression clouding your judgment.

Professor Roger Baker from Bournemouth University said that crying is the transformation of distress into something tangible, and the process itself reduces the feeling of stress. When someone tells you to "just let it out," you really should heed the advice!

Feeling and expressing emotion, whether it is crying or allowing yourself five minutes to be angry, are ways of facing emotions head-on. By expressing your emotions— crying, yelling into a pillow or empty room, taking a kickboxing class, or even writing poetry or journaling—you give yourself the mental space to move forward toward personal goals or solutions without the cloud of anxiety, anger, or stress hanging over your head.

Avoiding, suppressing, or ignoring emotions can have negative health consequences such as anxiety and depressive disorders. Some people even turn to compulsive behaviors such as alcoholism or drug abuse in lieu of allowing themselves to feel emotion.

The University of Texas psychologist James Pennebaker discovered that even putting feelings into words had a therapeutic and stress-relieving effect. He showed that expressively writing for 20 minutes per day helped people become less depressed, less anxious, and visit the doctor less frequently. In one portion of the study, Pennebaker took a group of recently laid-off software engineers. He had the participants write about their thoughts and feelings for 20 minutes per day. Remarkably, he discovered that the engineers who participated in his writing study were three times more likely to find new jobs than their peers who did not have emotional outlets to express themselves.

There are a number of ways to express your emotions, and the method that you choose doesn't matter. What does matter is that you are taking the time to feel your emotions to prevent them from intruding into your life and altering your decision-making ability. Both James Pennebaker and the APA showed that emotional expression is healthy and can give you a competitive edge over those who choose to suppress their emotions instead of feeling them. Mentally tough people know how to express their emotions and practice it as a skill that will increase their mental grit and flexibility.

Emotional Granularity

Since it is clear that emotional suppression is not the answer, what should you do instead? *Emotional granularity* is another part of the answer. This is the process of understanding what you are feeling by putting a specific name on it. It seems insignificant, but you will be able to release some of the intensity of the emotion just by allowing it to make itself known. There's a certain amount of tension from a lack of clarity about your feelings.

People that have finely tuned feelings and are very in touch with their emotions are said to exhibit emotional granularity. It's not about being able to complicatedly label every emotion you have or just expand your vocabulary so that you can do this. It is about experiencing the world, and thus yourself, more precisely. By doing this, you will be able to better identify what it is exactly that you're feeling, and by identifying it, you will be able to understand the reasoning behind it.

Emotional granularity was coined in the 1990s by Lisa Feldman Barrett, who asked hundreds of volunteers to track and monitor their emotional experiences for weeks or months. All the participants in the study used the same vocabulary to define their emotions with standard words such as "sad," "angry," and "afraid." However, the study found that some people used the words to refer to distinct and differing experiences. Each word represented multiple emotional concepts and feelings. Others in the study lumped these words together under a single conceptual meaning, basically alluding to the feelings of being miserable.

According to Barrett, the greater the granularity, the "more precisely" you can experience yourself and your world. This means that you can pinpoint how you feel and better identify a solution. By using different words for different emotions and individualizing your vocabulary, there are many more benefits to your emotional health. We become what we label ourselves, and this can either help or hurt you.

People who were able to learn diverse emotional concepts were able to understand more finely tailored emotions. Emotional granularity can have a large influence on your health and well-being because it equips your brain to handle a wider range of emotions that you may experience. In other words, by knowing what you're feeling, you know better what the causes and underlying emotional needs are, and you know how to solve it.

For example, you may be feeling a combination of sadness, boredom, restlessness, and yearning, and without the proper understanding of your emotions, you may just generalize it as feeling sad.

But this does not solve the problem because it may not be exactly what you're feeling. However, this all changes if you have emotional granularity and are able to correctly identify your emotion as loneliness. Lumping emotions together means that you may not know how to deal with them, but identifying them all as distinct, independent emotions promotes understanding. Acting to fix a general feeling of sadness is a far different course of action than acting to fix loneliness.

The better your understanding of what it is exactly that you're experiencing, the more flexibility your brain has in anticipating or prescribing actions. It is easy to generalize or dismiss what you are feeling, but it is much more effective to give it some thought and pinpoint exactly what your emotional state is.

One step to take in increasing your emotional vocabulary is to take a look at the true spectrum of emotions. Quick, try to name as many emotions as you can. How many did you come up with? Most psychologists identify either five to eight basic emotions.

However, psychologist Robert Plutchik put forth that there are 34,000 distinct emotions. Imagine how precise you can be in formulating your solution when you can define your emotions with such exactness.

Mental toughness typically conjures up an image of a stoic stiff upper lip, but that is far removed from reality. Feeling your emotions and truly understanding them gives you a proper foundation to take charge of your life.

Thinking Long-Term

Expressing your emotions is vital to mental health and resiliency. But there is another step that mentally tough people take to ensure they make balanced, well-thought-through decisions—they aren't reactive to what happens on a daily level. To be successful in regulating your emotions, your ability to think long-term instead of focusing on the day-to-day nitty-gritty of life will prove invaluable.

Many people make the mistake of spending too much of their time focused on the immediate future or sucked into the status quo. Instead, you should consciously choose to zoom out and look at the broader picture in order to gain control over your emotions. Focusing on small setbacks that occur in the short-term can skew your view of what matters in the long-term.

Let's pretend that you had set a goal to eat more whole foods and produce on a daily basis.

On Friday, you didn't manage to eat a salad with your lunch, and on Sunday you went out with friends and ate an entire plate of deep-fried Buffalo wings. Many people may focus on the short-term and berate themselves for making such poor choices in relation to their goal. However, by choosing to zoom out and look at the broader picture, these two examples may be only tiny blips on the radar. You only have cause for concern when there are numerous blips and a pattern begins to form.

No, you didn't meet your goal on Friday and Sunday, but perhaps when looking at the entire month it will become clear that you have been making great strides toward eating more whole foods and produce on a daily basis. When looking at a single day, small deviations from your goal may loom large and seem like overwhelming setbacks. However, when viewing your choices for an entire month the true impact of an occasional small daily setback will become clear. A small setback on the daily scale does not derail a long-term goal.

By simply adjusting your perspective, you are able to identify small setbacks, such as eating a plate of wings with your friends, and move on much more quickly and with less stress and negativity. In general, if an event will seem unimportant or forgettable in a few days then it is not worth holding on to or dwelling on.

Choosing to focus on the immediate moment causes you to engage with life in a very reactive manner: you are emotional; prone to making quick, ill-thought-through decisions; and easily derailed by day-to-day setbacks. Instead of living in this reactive manner, those with mental toughness make a conscious choice to live their lives in a state of controlled deliberateness. They are logical, measured, and consider the long-term implications of their decision before setting a course of action. Everyone encounters day-to-day ups and downs, but obsessing over short-term wins or losses is a waste of energy.

Olympic athletes are a fantastic example of individuals who shrug off short-term wins or losses to remain fixated on their long-term goals. Whether an athlete encounters a minor injury, a first-place trophy in a national competition, or unexpected training challenges, the long-term goal does not change. These small occurrences hold little weight in the face of an Olympic medal two or three years in the future. Resilient, strong individuals know that you must focus on what you can control each day, put in the hard work to move toward your goals, and live your life in a controlled, deliberate manner.

To further contrast the difference between living your life in an emotional, reactionary manner and choosing to be controlled and deliberate, consider the following scenario:

> You have $86,400 in your checking account. While getting into your car one evening, a thief approaches and robs you. He manages to steal $10 from your wallet. Would you spend your remaining $86,390 hiring private investigators and lawyers to find and prosecute the thief? Or

would you recognize that in the long-term $10 means very little to you, and it is better to appreciate the events that have gone well in your life and move on from this small setback?

In this scenario, choosing to find and prosecute the thief would be an example of emotional and reactionary living. It may feel good in the short-term to give in to your emotions, especially because this event might seem huge when zoomed into your timeline of the day, but it ultimately squanders your time and can negatively impact your ability to attain your long-term goals. Instead, those with mental resiliency and strength choose to think long-term.

They zoom out on their timeline and take into account what $10, a small amount of money, truly means when considering the full amount they have in their checking account. They understand that it is a waste to spend the remaining $86,390 and instead choose to move on from this short-term setback and continue making progress toward their goals.

Some of you may have made the connection that there are 86,400 seconds in one day. This scenario can also be viewed in the context of a single day. Should you waste an entire day focusing on one 10-second setback? Of course not! That would be just as wasteful as squandering $86,390. When thinking about this 10 seconds or $10 in the future, it will seem inconsequential. A small setback, when you zoom out on your timeline, becomes recognizable for what it is—insignificant.

Humans are evolutionarily hardwired to react emotionally. Emotions are immediate and reactionary. To live in a controlled and deliberate manner requires logic. Due to our evolutionary hardwiring, it can take time for logical thought to be restored after an emotional setback. It is physically impossible for reactive emotions and logical thought to be occurring simultaneously within our brains.

Therefore, mentally resilient individuals choose to take some time before reacting to setbacks. This allows their brains time to process through the emotional reaction and move back into logical thought before making any decisions or taking action. Never react immediately. Always allow yourself time to calm down and clearly think through decisions or actions before committing yourself.

To master these skills, zoom out and look at the broader picture. Day-to-day wins or setbacks are inconsequential when viewed on a broader scale. Always choose to live your life with controlled deliberateness instead of allowing yourself to inhabit a short-term reactionary space. And ensure that after emotional setbacks, you allow yourself time to calm down and let your brain settle back into logical thought before committing to a course of action.

A final way to think long-term is to travel through time and think in terms of 10-10-10. The next time you feel you're about to lose your mental fortitude and give in, stop and try to transport yourself 10 minutes, 10 hours, and 10 days from the current moment. The idea is to disconnect from the emotional present by thinking about a time when you are calm and unaffected.

This may not seem so powerful, but it forces you to think specifically about your future self, specifically the future self that you are aspiring to. In the next 10 minutes, hours, and days, you want to view yourself as emotionally even and balanced. A lot of times, we may know that we are doing something harmful in the moment, but that's not enough to stop us from doing it because we don't have any connection to our future self that will have to deal with the consequences.

Someone has just cut you off in traffic and almost caused you to crash. There was no damage done, but you are livid and on the verge of chasing them down in your car and assaulting them. What if you were to think about your mental state in 10 minutes, hours, and days? Think about what you'll be doing, what you would be feeling if the event didn't occur, and where you would be.

In a sense, you are distracting yourself from the current emotional moment by reminding yourself that you have a life to live, and your current rage will keep you from doing that. Control your emotions by looking ahead to the rest of your life and visualizing how you want it to go.

There is an old Zen saying: "Your anger, depression, spite, or despair, so seemingly real and important right now; where will they have gone in a month, a week, or even a moment?"

Intense emotions blind us to the future and con us that now is all that matters. In fact, when we are incredibly angry or anxious, we can even forget that there is even going to *be* a future. We've all said or done things we later regret simply because, for a time, we let ourselves be dictated by our own emotion. Look beyond the immediate and you'll see the bigger picture and calm down, too.

The ABC Loop

The previous section was about zooming out and considering the bigger picture to remain calm and balanced. Another way to keep your mental toughness is to analyze the circumstances surrounding your emotions to understand what your triggers are. This is known as the ABC loop and it asks you to consider emotional reactions as the end result of a series of events.

The ABC loop is a classic behavioral therapy technique that considers all the elements that contribute to an emotional reaction. It stands for Antecedent, Behavior, and Consequence. The middle section, the behavior, is often called the Behavior of Interest, and the technique works by looking at the before and after to understand why the behavior in the middle occurred. It's also what you want to examine and regulate or control—hence, the increased scrutiny on it. To control the behavior, you must understand and control the antecedent and consequence.

Let's begin with Antecedent. This is the environment, the events, or the preceding the Behavior of Interest. This is your cause or trigger, typically. Anything that happens before the event that may contribute to the behavior would fall into this category. When identifying the antecedents, consider where and when it is occurring, during what activity, with whom it occurred, and what any others were doing at the time.

For example, perhaps you are someone who finds yourself constantly arguing with your parents. You might realize that most of the time you don't even agree with what you're arguing with, but you do it anyway. You want to stop this behavior, so you think about the last time it occurred. Set the scene first. In this situation: dinner at your parents' house, early afternoon, things were going fine, you were talking about your job and your career goals. This is the Antecedent.

Then we move onto the Behavior, which is the focus of this technique. This is what follows the antecedent and is what you have identified as something to change or control. In this case, the behavior is uncontrollable anger toward the people around you, which causes stress and conflict. It is important to describe the behavior in full when looking back in hindsight. In this situation, there are raised voices, dramatic gestures, insults thrown, and intentionally vicious comments being said, most of which were irrelevant to the actual argument.

Last is the Consequence of the behavior. This outcome is important because it is often one that reinforces the behavior. If the consequence is one that is genuinely undesirable, most unwanted behaviors will not be repeated, but if there is some sort of reward that is incidentally received, then the behavior will continue. In this case, the outcome may be that one of your parents, usually your mother, leaves the room upset and the dinner is cut short, whereby you then go home. This is not that negative of a consequence, and thus, the behavior sees no real reason to change. Consider, instead, if the reaction was being kicked out of your parents' home and becoming homeless. The behavior would certainly have reason to change.

Let's take a deeper look at how these all work together. The Antecedent, as mentioned before, is the family dinner. It is important to mention the last thing to happen before the behavior. In this case, it was questions about career goals and aspirations. Considering this is the last casual question before the argument, it is clear that this is the catalyst. If you are looking back at your own event and are able to identify the catalyst, consider why it affects you so much. Do you always react in the same way? If you can identify what it is that catalyzes a behavior you want to stop, then you can focus on it and actively try to redirect your behavior when you encounter a similar situation again.

The next thing to observe is the behavior itself. In this case, it is uncontrollable yelling, but it can be a whole range of different ones. Think about why it is that you choose this behavior. In this case, maybe you feel as if you're not being heard. Maybe you want to exercise some control or authority or overcompensate because you are feeling cornered. Whatever the reasoning behind it, think about if there is another way to release your emotions without that behavior—even if it is something as simple as taking a moment to calm down, leaving the situation, or telling someone that you are not in an emotional state to continue. Find a way to redirect your emotions so that you produce a different behavior.

The last thing to consider is the consequence. If it is a recurring behavior, then that must mean you get some reward out of it. You get your way in some way or another, either because you enjoy creating conflict, or yelling and anger allow you to continually avoid harsh conversations. In this scenario, your mother has left the scene directly after the argument and you are forced to go home. Maybe this is exactly what you want—to spend less time with your parents. Maybe you just want them to support your career, and when it seems they aren't, then you don't wish to be there anymore. Whatever the case, this isn't a consequence that will force you to change.

The ABC loop is designed so that you can focus on the before and after of a behavior and figure out why certain behaviors are being repeated over and over again. If you can identify the cause and the effect of a behavior, you can better control your emotional reactions by avoiding those triggering causes or by considering the reward you are unconsciously receiving from emotional outbursts.

In other words, take a step or two backward. Ask yourself, "How did I get here?" Understanding where our emotions arise from and what evokes them is a crucial component to help you begin to manage emotions. When you notice your emotions, be willing to hunt for the triggers that may have propelled you into your given feelings. Then fast-forward and ask yourself about the consequences of your actions. Emotions don't happen in a vacuum. You are ultimately responsible for them, but part of mental toughness is understanding where they stem from and cutting off their supply.

Takeaways:

- Ultimately, we are all slaves to our emotions. This is an undeniable fact. But at least we can try to battle our lesser instincts and think with logic and reason.
- First, it is important to note that this does not mean suppressing your emotions. In fact, expressing them has been shown to have huge psychological benefits. The more specific and granular you can be with your emotions, the bigger the benefits. It's just a matter of moderation between remaining in control and *feeling*.
- Thinking long-term is a powerful means of remaining calm and rational. When something goes wrong, it may feel like the end of the world, but then what happens when you zoom out? On a long enough timeline, nothing is really very serious. The problem is, we all live in the

present moment, but if we were to adjust our expectations and think long-term, we'd understand that we rarely have anything to truly worry about.

- Sometimes when we're emotional, we forget there is going to be a future. Remind yourself by thinking in terms of 10-10-10 and looking toward the rest of your life.
- Finally, a way to build mental toughness and rein in your emotions is to use the ABC loop. ABC stands for Antecedent, Behavior, and Consequence, and they all work together to either reinforce or punish behaviors such as emotional reactions.

Chapter 4. Distorted Realities

Our perception of the world is 99% incorrect. There's no other way around it. What we see is often not the reality that exists, and that's completely normal.

This is because of the various biases and perspectives we bring from our past. Unfortunately, in general, these misperceptions make us feel weak and disempowered. For instance, we may unfairly compare ourselves to others or focus on the most negative aspects of a situation—a suspicion that a spouse or partner is cheating due to a grueling work schedule. There is obviously another explanation, but the perception is there nonetheless.

To become mentally tough, you must change the way that you view the world. Information and events come to us in a neutral state; it is only through our interpretation that these items have positive or negative connotations. How we choose to view events determines our realities and has the ability to completely undermine your resilience and will to persevere.

A *cognitive distortion* is a view of reality that is negative, pessimistic, and generally incorrect. It can damage your self-esteem, lower your confidence, and make you feel as if you have no control over your life. Cognitive distortion is also a form of self-talk that is extremely damaging to people. This form of self-talk can become so ingrained and habit-forming that people don't realize they are creating a sad version of reality and interpreting events in a completely negative manner.

Cognitive distortions directly undermine our mental toughness because they make us battle a fantasy world where the odds are stacked against us. Most of us have enough trouble with reality; distorting our view of the world to be more menacing and difficult just saps our mental toughness unnecessarily.

While returning from the restroom, Craig walked past a closed-door meeting in Max, his supervisor's, office. As he passed by the glass door, he noticed that almost all of his coworkers were in the room and many glanced in his direction.

He immediately began to feel nervous. Were they talking about him? Had he done something wrong? He was probably going to be fired! Last week, he noticed Sheila and Katie giggling and looking at him in the break room. And the Nickerby account had just moved to another company. He was probably going to get fired, and it would be impossible to find another job because he would definitely be getting a horrible recommendation. He wouldn't be able to make his truck payment next month without a job; it would probably get repossessed.

Craig was in a downward spiral for the rest of the day, worrying about his future work prospects and how he would survive without his usual income while looking for a new job.

The next morning was Craig's birthday, and he was feeling very depressed. He dragged himself into work, prepared for the worst. As soon as he sat down at his desk he heard a loud "Surprise! Happy Birthday, Craig!" All of his coworkers were gathered behind his desk, armed with small gifts. Sheila rushed over and blurted out, "We've been planning this surprise for weeks! We thought we had been caught when you walked past Max's office yesterday, but it looks like we really surprised you."

Craig was suffering from severe cognitive distortion.

His perception of an event, a meeting of many of his coworkers, was colored by his negative viewpoint. Although his coworkers were ultimately planning a surprise birthday party, Craig jumped to conclusions and assumed the worst. This cognitive distortion served to lower Craig's self-esteem and put him into a panic mode in which he wasted his energy and time worried about an unlikely future scenario. Mentally tough people know how to identify and disarm cognitive distortions; letting these types of thoughts inhabit your mind drains your mental toughness.

What Are Cognitive Distortions?

In 1976, psychologist Aaron Beck was the first to propose the theory behind cognitive distortions. It wasn't until the 1980s that David Burns popularized it with common names and examples of the distortions. Cognitive distortions are the ways in which your mind convinces you of something that isn't true. They are usually used to reinforce pessimistic thinking or negative emotions, and we often tell ourselves things that sound rational and accurate yet only serve to emphasize our self-doubt or lack of confidence. Cognitive distortions are at the core of what cognitive-behavioral therapists try to teach a client to change in psychotherapy.

The first step to launching a counterattack on these negative thoughts is by noticing when you are having them. Then you must make a conscious effort to turn them off or find alternative explanations for your worries. By refuting or turning off this negative thinking over and over again, the negative thoughts will diminish over time and automatically be replaced by more rational, balanced thinking. It is only through constant vigilance that you can replace the bad habit of cognitive distortion with the good habit of positive thinking.

Many of us may notice this type of internal dialogue while at work. A nagging thought telling you you're inferior to your colleagues based on their level of education in comparison to yours, a worry about your public speaking skills before a big meeting, or a concern that your boss prefers to give big projects to your coworkers are all examples of cognitive distortions.

All three worries are negative thoughts that likely have no basis in reality. Choosing to stop these thoughts and give them a more positive spin will eventually cause them to be replaced by more logical and balanced thinking.

Mentally tough individuals know that to perceive reality clearly and without unnecessary emotional turmoil they have to turn off the pessimistic or negative cognitive distortions. This allows for clear, logical thought and advancement in the workplace, socially, and in relationships.

Types of Cognitive Distortions

All-or-Nothing Thinking

"Gosh, I haven't read a single book this month and my goal was to read three! I'm horrible at sticking to goals. If I can't read three books, I may as well not read at all."

"Corey chews with his mouth open. How have I never realized this?! How disgusting. I can't imagine being with someone who chews with his mouth open for the rest of my life. He must not be 'the one.'"

All-or-nothing thinking can also be called tunnel vision. This type of cognitive distortion occurs when you only focus on the good or the bad, instead of taking a balanced viewpoint on life events and situations. There is only black and white, which causes you to severely overreact either way.

As fictional race car driver Ricky Bobby in *Talladega Nights* said, "If you ain't first, you're last." Obviously, there are many positions between first and last. Although earning second or third place isn't ideal, there is a huge difference between running a 2:19 marathon and a 4:12. It's vital to not lose sight of the middle ground because all-or-nothing thinking destroys resilience. The world is rarely over, and consequences that seem enormous and irreversible rarely are.

By focusing only on the extremes of good and bad, you lose sight of the bigger picture. A characteristic of mentally tough individuals is their ability to zoom out and look at the goals and events in their lives in a larger scale. By getting caught up in all-or-nothing thinking, this sort of large-scale view is lost and small issues can suddenly feel greatly magnified.

All-or-nothing thinking also manifests itself through lists of ironclad rules about behavior or expectations. People who break these rules make us feel angry, and in turn, if we break a rule, we feel guilty. Lists of 'shoulds' or 'musts' such as "I must go to the gym every day" or "I must arrive at work at least 15 minutes before my shift begins" might sound motivational, but they leave little room for compromise or adjustment if life events get in the way of your plan.

All of these tendencies create a set of expectations that you are destined to fall short of. And when this happens on a continual basis, you can't help but feel inadequate and mediocre at best.

To overcome the cognitive distortion of all-or-nothing thinking, you must challenge yourself to see the middle ground. You should take into account other viewpoints and strive to see different interpretations of the situation. What does your best friend or father think? What other solutions or ways to approach the problem can you envision? Can you list three positives to balance out the negatives you've fixated on thus far?

Push yourself to think outside of the box to come up with as many interpretations as possible. Even if they seem wacky, having more options forces you to think outside of the cognitive distortion. When everything seems bleak and negative, this realization will cause you to be a bit kinder to yourself.

"Ultimately, it is better to read one or two books than it is to read nothing. Maybe I'll just start with one chapter tonight and see what happens."

"Corey has so many admirable qualities; that's why I fell in love with him. Chewing with his mouth open is really a pretty minor problem."

Personalizing

"Why can't Marsha hold down a job? She is constantly moving from company to company. I think she was even fired from this last position. I must have done something wrong as a parent. If only we had sent her to Laurelswood high school instead of the public school, this never would have happened! It's all my fault. I should have quit my job and just been there for her."

"I feel terrible that Patricia overcooked the pot roast. If only Jeremy and I hadn't been 30 minutes late for the dinner party. If only I had told him to hurry this, wouldn't have happened! I take full responsibility for this. I should have cooked everything myself."

Personalization is the mother of guilt. In the cognitive distortion of personalizing, you feel responsible for events that cannot conceivably be your fault. While it is admirable to take responsibility for your actions, there are things that are completely out of your control: the subway schedule, other people, and a million day-to-day factors.

While engaging in personalizing, you might believe that everything others say or do is a direct personal reaction to you even when logically this doesn't fit. Personalizing directly impacts mental toughness; you cannot focus on reaching your goals and being mentally resilient when you are hyper-focused on others. To be mentally tough you have to be able to focus on yourself and improving your life, not on the perceived reactions of others. It's tough for you to stand strong in the face of adversity if you believe that you are responsible for all of it.

The opposite of personalizing is *externalizing*. It is another important cognitive distortion to note. When caught in this trap, individuals refuse to blame themselves for anything; instead, they blame everyone and everything else. These individuals blame others for holding them back, causing them pain or sadness, and even point to others as the cause of life troubles. All of this blame is given without any recognition for the part that the individual played in his or her own troubles, pain, or sadness.

In order to escape from both of these cognitive distortions, question what part you actually played in the event and consider options in which you are not entirely to blame.

Were you truly the main actor in the event or did you just play a supporting role? If the blame was shifted to another actor, how might the event play out? Did you do the best you could? What were your intentions or motives? What would you change if you went back in time? How much of the situation could you truly control or influence?

By going through this mental rehearsal you will be able to identify your true role in the event and the most likely person or thing that is actually at fault. More importantly, you'll gain a balanced view of situations so you can withstand them better.

"Marsha received a good education. Maybe she hasn't found a job that fulfills her yet. I did the best I could with what I knew at the time."

"Patricia didn't actually wait for us to arrive to serve the pot roast. Maybe our late arrival was just a coincidence. I have to admit, she has never been the best cook."

Overgeneralization

"I'm never going to find a girlfriend because my last date went so terribly! I am destined to be single forever."

"He will never be on time. He was late for both of our previous meetings. He's a lost cause. I am not going to meet with him again."

In the trap of *overgeneralization,* you take one or two negative experiences and assume all future similar experiences will be negative. Overgeneralization is unrepresentative of reality because you are operating on minimal experience, information, and evidence. You are jumping to conclusions and constructing a world that doesn't exist in reality, just in your limited exposure.

Common cues of overgeneralization are "always" and "never." When starting a sentence or a thought with "always" or "never," consider whether you have the experience or evidence to back up the statement. Do you have the ability to look past your current emotional feelings or the most recent event that is causing you to feel this way? The very nature of emotions is to overwhelm and cloud judgment—perhaps you are merely honoring your emotions instead of seeking a balanced view.

Overgeneralization is common in relationships and in the work environment. Often, past hurt or disappointment clouds your ability to envision a positive future. As we know from the past chapter, being pragmatically optimistic is an important skill to build mental toughness. Overgeneralization has a direct negative impact on your ability to remain optimistic.

To overcome the trap of overgeneralization, take time to question whether evidence exists showing that future events could be different. Consider just how little information you have. Has every event of this type in your life ended in exactly the same way, or are there more than a few outliers? Do all of your friends have the exact same story, or have some of them had different experiences?

Would you feel differently when you're further removed from a situation and unemotional? Are you jumping to conclusions in a defensible way? If you believe that A + B = C, are A and B present, and is C a definite conclusion?

"Sure, Abby rejected me, but I've only been single for two months. Maybe I need a little

more time to find someone more compatible."

"He was late for our two previous meetings, but there has been a lot of construction on Laurel Ave. He might have just gotten caught up in the construction traffic last week."

Catastrophizing

"Lacy is out late again. I just know that she's cheating on me! We're never going to last as a couple; we have to be heading for divorce. I need to call a lawyer right now."

"Why haven't I received a letter from the University of California yet? They must be rejecting me. I can't believe it! I'm not going to get into any universities. What am I going to do? I guess I need to start learning how to become a plumber."

When you engage in *catastrophizing*, you immediately jump to the worst-case scenario and lose hope because the event seems so imminent. This is when you leap into an assumption with little to no evidence. This is a thinking trap!

Mental toughness requires optimism and a belief that your actions can positively impact your future. By engaging in catastrophizing, you are limiting your ability to prepare for the future and take action to reach your goals.

Catastrophizing can cause you to become stressed and anxious. How tough can you really be if every day you appear to be facing your own personal version of the apocalypse?

As with other cognitive distortions, a degree of introspection and thinking about your thoughts is necessary. Question whether things are truly as bad as you are making them seem. Consider alternative explanations and past experiences in similar situations. What are the positive aspects of the event? In past similar situations, what did I do and how did the event turn out? How would an innocent bystander explain the situation? What am I fixating on and why?

Perhaps most importantly, what does this say about me and my insecurities?

"Maybe Lacy is just working late; she mentioned a big work project when she was late last Wednesday. Oh, here's a text from her right now."

"The University of California said letters could arrive anytime this week. It's only Monday... Maybe a letter will come tomorrow."

Magnifying and Minimizing

"I'm so awful at writing legal briefs. Why can't I ever get this formatting right? I missed two punctuation errors in that 50-page document. I'm trash."

"My puff pastry is the best of any of the chefs at Le Petit Poulet. My pastry cups are always perfectly formed and golden-brown. None of that matters. I'm still horrible."

Magnifying is choosing to focus on negative aspects of a situation or event until they seem to be the most important part. When engaging in the cognitive distortion of magnifying, you may focus on only parts of your body, aspects of your personality, or work traits that you view as negative while overlooking all of the other traits that are positive. Even if you've accomplished something great, you can't help but nitpick and see your victory in a negative light. It's as if you are wearing glasses that only allow you to see flaws and faults, no matter how small.

Minimizing is the opposite. This cognitive distortion occurs when you minimize positive events, aspects, or traits. While engaging in minimizing, you end up with the same view as when you magnify— nothing is good enough, and you are inadequate. Take the same victory and you will downplay your accomplishments as unimportant and luck-based. You can do nothing right; it is mediocre at best.

You simply view yourself or your actions as flawed instead of taking a more realistic view. While engaging in the cognitive distortion of magnifying and minimizing, you ignore your positive attributes and fixate only on the negatives while doing the opposite for someone else. You may view your strengths in a way that makes them look inconsequential while highly praising the same strengths of a coworker or friend. Both of these cognitive distortions cause you to view things in an unbalanced, unrealistic way.

To be mentally tough, it is important to view the world realistically. By magnifying or minimizing negatives, your outlook becomes skewed and you are not able to make logical, well-considered decisions.

To overcome the trap of magnifying negativity, challenge yourself to notice your positive attributes, list your strengths, and brainstorm reasons that you are deserving of praise or respect. Is this negative aspect a small detail or a large part of the event?

What are some of the positive things about me or this event?

To overcome the cognitive distortion of minimizing positivity, do the same. Understand that you are capable and impactful.

"My formatting might not be perfect, but I always have the best phrasing and perfectly edited briefs. And really, I know my boss finds my formatting nicer than most of the other paralegals."

Jumping to Conclusions

"Why didn't David smile back at me this morning? He must think the project proposal I sent him yesterday afternoon is stupid!"

"There's no point in even going to the gym. I'm never going to reach my goal of running that 10k with Candace."

Jumping to conclusions occurs when you make an irrational assumption about people or circumstances based on personal opinion and feeling. It begins with feelings of inadequacy or insecurity, which influence the way you perceive events and statements. When you observe something that confirms your worst fears, you take it as a confirmation of everything you secretly knew to be terrible and true. Just like with other cognitive distortions, it causes you to fall down a rabbit hole of negativity until you end up at the worst possible conclusion.

There are two categories within the cognitive distortion of jumping to conclusions: mind-reading and fortune-telling.

While engaging in mind-reading, you assume you know what someone else is thinking. It is impossible to know exactly what someone else is thinking, yet with this cognitive distortion, people make decisions based on the imagined thoughts of other people. And of course, people are always thinking the worst about you.

Fortune-telling involves predicting negative future events without evidence. When engaging in fortune-telling, you predict only negative things for the future and have no real basis for doing so. Mentally tough people understand the importance of being realistically optimistic; fortune-telling makes this impossible.

Building toughness for the future and taking steps toward reaching your goals requires the ability to think realistically and plan specifically. You cannot be realistic or make useful plans if you are basing your thoughts off of hastily made conclusions.

To stop jumping to conclusions, question whether other explanations for events are possible or whether additional options exist. How else could you view this situation? If you believe in a certain conclusion, what are the pieces of evidence to support that? What other conclusions are more likely or common?

"David looked a little distracted. Maybe he didn't notice me smiling at him."

"If I go to the gym today, maybe I'll get a little closer to being ready to run the 10k. And if not, at least we can still switch to the 5k option."

Emotional Reasoning

"I can't afford to pay all of my bills again this month. I feel hopeless and depressed. There is no solution to my problems."

"Oh my gosh, why did I bring up that movie!? It's 10 years old; everyone will think I'm so out of touch. I'm such a bore at all these parties."

Engaging in the cognitive distortion of emotional reasoning means that you are taking your emotions as evidence. Whatever you feel right now is whatever reality you find yourself in. That's a difficult way to live.

While engaging in this behavior, observed evidence is discarded in favor of the "truth" of your feelings about the event. Humans tend to believe that how they feel must automatically be true. If you feel stupid and boring, then you must actually be stupid and boring. This is commonly referenced by the phrase "I feel it; therefore, it must be true."

Emotional reasoning is one of the most dangerous of the cognitive distortions because it can be so wildly different from reality and in the span of minutes can change. Is reality actually changing moment by moment? Of course not! Only your emotions are changing that quickly.

Falling into the trap of emotional reasoning is different than the previously discussed skills of controlling your emotions and regulating how you choose to express them.

Being conscious of and allowing yourself to feel your emotions is important to maintaining your mental health and growing mental toughness; however, that does not mean that you should take your emotions to heart as a true expression of reality. In fact, your emotions often have very little to do with the status quo of reality. Remember, reality is often very neutral, yet your emotions cause you to perceive reality as either positive or negative. Many psychologists believe that emotional reasoning originates from negative thoughts and should be viewed as an uncontrolled or automatic response.

To escape the trap of emotional reasoning and take control of this "automatic response," question whether your emotional state of mind is preventing you from viewing events clearly. Just like you wouldn't go grocery shopping when starving, you shouldn't evaluate anything when emotional. Always take time to return to a calm state before making decisions or committing yourself to a specific course of action. Do you feel bad about yourself or the situation at hand?

Viewing a situation while emotional, or with emotional reasoning, is like watching a completely neutral scene with horror music being played over it. And then joyous music. And then the next minute, music fitting for a clown's entrance. You won't know what's really happening in front of your face because the music will influence you a certain way. Finally, ensure that you are experiencing your emotions but do not assume that your feelings are directly connected to reality.

"It is really upsetting to not have enough money, but that doesn't mean I can't find a solution. Maybe I should look into a side job. I know Maggie was talking about a great new tutoring client she found... I might be able to find a new client, too."

"That one statement might have been kind of boring. But I know that Mark thought our conversation about the new Korean restaurant was interesting. Just because I thought something I said was boring doesn't actually mean that everyone thinks I am boring."

Takeaways:

- What is a cognitive distortion? It is a pattern of thinking that is

118

unrepresentative of reality. This is significant because most cognitive distortions arc disempowering and cause you to doubt yourself, lose confidence, and lose mental toughness. How can you be mentally tough if the world seems to be pitted against you? You're just starting from a place where you can't win.

- Cognitive distortions are often automatic thought patterns that arise from our own insecurities and fears. They aren't totally unfounded, but they depart wildly from reality. They are characterized by jumping to conclusions based on assumptions and incomplete information, as well as overreactions.

- A few of the most well-known and dangerous cognitive distortions are all-or-nothing thinking, personalizing, overgeneralizing, catastrophizing, magnifying and minimizing, and jumping to conclusions. An especially notable cognitive distortion that robs us of resilience is emotional reasoning. This is when reality is defined by the emotions we feel at that very moment.

Chapter 5. Build the Skill

Chloe recently found herself in a new relationship. Zack seemed great, but he lived a very different lifestyle than Chloe. Chloe was very involved in her local yoga studio. She believed that eating mindfully and practicing yoga on a daily basis was important. Zack didn't share the same beliefs; he was a video game developer who spent a lot of time working on his products and nothing else.

Over the first few months of their relationship, Chloe began attending classes at her local yoga studio less frequently. Zack always wanted her to spend the night at his place, and it was a long drive back to catch the 6:30 a.m. class. Since she was spending the night at Zack's more frequently, she also ate a lot of meals with him. He was a real carnivore and one of his favorite things to do on a Friday night was get some burgers from a local food truck and test out one of his newly released games. Chloe loved the indulgent feeling that came from relaxing on Zack's couch.

Eventually, Chloe found herself gaining weight and she began to feel less balanced. She felt less patient, and she began to experience mood swings. It was around the six-month mark of their relationship that Chloe realized something needed to change. She had strayed far from her practice of mindful eating and she realized she hadn't been to a single yoga class in almost two weeks.

Chloe decided she needed to stop making excuses.

Of course it felt great to eat burgers and sleep in, but doing so on a regular basis was taking a toll on her mental and physical well-being. She vowed to get up on time to attend yoga classes and cook with Zack more frequently. By choosing to avoid the trap of instant gratification, Chloe was able to return to a comfortable compromise. She could spend time with Zack while still taking care of her own mental, emotional, and physical health.

Mental toughness is not simply a trait you are born with. It is a skill that needs to be cultivated and developed. Mental toughness is like a muscle that needs to be focused on and worked in order to grow. As Chloe found, it is easier to allow your mental toughness to fade than it is to continue to practice self-discipline. However, by making yourself do the tenth rep instead of stopping at nine, choosing to ask the extra question when it would be easier to accept the original answer, or deciding to tackle the bigger project at work, you can actively exercise your mental toughness muscle and keep it in shape.

So often we think that mental toughness is about how we respond in extreme situations, but what about day-to-day challenges? Grit is a trait that can and should be applied every day. Prove to yourself that you have enough grit to get into the ring and do battle with life!

To build your mental toughness muscle, you need to tackle small things every day. You have to build up the muscle and then put in the work to keep it growing every day. You have to move out of your comfort zone. No one becomes tough doing things they like.

UFC light heavyweight Quinton Jackson said, "Toughness is a skill. You learn it. Nobody comes… born that tough. That's why we do stuff like those sand-dune runs. It's a very conscious thing we do, and it's to take people out of their comfort zones, break them down, and positively build them a structure that will help them when times are rough."

Retired UFC fighter Brian Stann still forces himself to do things he calls "unpleasant" to ensure he doesn't lose his edge. Some of these unpleasant things occur during his workouts, but others are as simple as proving he can survive on very little sleep even when he doesn't need to.

Sand-dune runs or getting into the habit of voluntarily choosing to do "unpleasant" things can help increase toughness. It is through the daily habit of choosing the unpleasant or uncomfortable that you discipline your mind. By choosing the uncomfortable, everything that comes later in the day, even things that you would normally dread, seem easier. By doing this consistently, you are preparing yourself to overcome anything that life can throw at you.

Toughness needs to be practiced. A recent study from the University of Miami focused on mindfulness training and its impact on student athletes. Mindfulness training is about focusing on the present moment and observing your thoughts and feelings without judgment.

It was shown that adherence to a mindfulness training program protected the student athletes' attention spans and prevented a decline in well-being, even during stressful preseason training. The results pointed to continuous practice of the techniques as being key to the outcome. Consistency is key to improve mental toughness, whether it is through thinking long-term, practicing realistic optimism, or avoiding cognitive distortions. Mentally tough individuals know that in order to see results, they must be diligent in their practice of key skills that contribute to mental toughness.

"The hallmarks of elite performance within the most hostile environments are the ability to be tough-minded, adjust to unpredictable demands, and to properly attend to the task at hand," said Michael Garvais, a high-performance psychology coach advising the study.

Building the skill of mental toughness is about the mindsets we've discussed so far, but it's also about engaging in acts to purposely build and enhance it. Achieving true mental toughness takes consistent action over time, not just wishes.

Facing the Uncomfortable

There are some specific evidence-based practices that you can undertake to enhance your mental toughness. By controlling and mastering these small, everyday situations you will gain the confidence to excel in even the most unpleasant of future situations.

The first example is taking cold showers. Taking cold showers in the morning is unpleasant, but there are immense benefits to cold-water exposure, including a stronger immune system, better blood circulation, and reduced inflammation. Forcing yourself to take cold showers makes you more disciplined, and doing this every day develops mental toughness and willpower. Plus, everything else that happens in your day will seem so much easier because you've already accomplished a difficult task!

Taking cold showers will force you to become comfortable being uncomfortable. This eventually allows you to dwell in uncomfortable states for as long as your willpower can take it. This increased willpower can transfer into the office or even the gym.

There are two parts to adapting to the cold: the physical and the mental. On a purely physical level, your body has to adapt to the lower temperature. This is the easy part. From a mental standpoint, your mind will try to fight back against the unpleasantness. If you listen to your own inner voice of self-doubt and give in to the desire for comfort, then you won't be able to muster enough courage or willpower in other, easier situations. You ultimately have to realize that a daily cold shower isn't going to harm you; it will make you better and stronger.

Another act of daily discipline to engage in is refusing to hit the snooze alarm. Small wins can set the tone of your day, and this is actually the first moment of your day.

Developing discipline is about doing the little things right, consistently.

It's tempting to hit your snooze button in the morning, especially when there is nothing forcing you to wake up at that time. But it's a decisive moment that can determine the outcome of your entire day. Use it as an opportunity to exercise your discipline and again tackle the unpleasant.

Jocko Willink, a retired U.S. Navy SEAL and author of *Extreme Ownership: How US Navy SEALs Lead and Win*, explains, "Discipline starts every day when the first alarm clock goes off in the morning. I say 'first alarm clock' because I have three... That way, there is no excuse for not getting out of bed, especially with all that rests on that *decisive moment...* the moment the alarm goes off is the first test; it sets the tone for the rest of the day. The test is not a complex one: when the alarm goes off, do you get up out of bed, or do you lie there in comfort and fall back asleep? If you have the discipline to get out of bed, you win—you pass the test. If you are mentally weak for that moment and you let that weakness keep you in bed, you fail. Though it seems small, that weakness translates to more significant decisions. But if you exercise discipline, that, too, translates to more substantial elements of your life."

Jocko Willink it telling us that choosing to be disciplined in small ways can have huge payoffs. Small acts of discipline can quickly build into larger and larger acts and eventually lead to whatever level of disciplined lifestyle you want to achieve. This discipline and self-control directly translates into mental toughness. If you can get directly out of bed without hitting the snooze or take a cold shower, then you can master that difficult client or swim that extra lap.

A third example of discipline that you could engage in is to eat a raw clove of garlic every day. It's an overall healthy practice, yet it requires a degree of discipline. For those that have tried, this can be like eating a hot pepper in its harshness on the taste buds.

Some people choose to mix the garlic clove with yogurt, grate it into tea, or simply swallow it whole. However you choose to consume it, garlic has many positive health benefits, including high levels of magnesium, vitamin B6, and vitamin C. It also boosts the immune system and studies have shown that daily garlic supplementation reduces the frequency and duration of the common cold.

Amazingly, garlic can even reduce blood pressure and may reduce the risk of heart disease. All of these benefits can be obtained by simply including garlic in your daily routine. But the taste of raw garlic is off-putting to many, which is where the self-discipline comes in. Although the act of eating a daily clove of garlic may seem painful, it can make you better and stronger by increasing your discipline and self-control. These small daily acts add up to increasing your discipline "stamina."

Something as small as taking a cold shower, refusing to hit the snooze button, or eating a daily raw clove of garlic might seem inconsequential, but doing all the right little things can lead to doing the right big things. There is nothing forcing you to make these choices; it's all internal drive, self-control, and discipline. By choosing to do these unpleasant things on a daily basis you are preparing yourself for the real challenges and obstacles that you will face in life. Make a statement; attack the day head-on. These are just ideas for how to start building your toughness muscle; all you need to do is grow an indifference to discomfort and unpleasantness.

Practice Delaying Gratification

Humans are hardwired to want things immediately. This is called instant gratification and it is an extremely powerful force that winds its way through all aspects of life. It's one of the most universal and predictable causes for human behavior.

In most psychological models, humans are believed to act upon the *pleasure principle*. This principle is the driving force that implores you to satisfy your needs, wants, and urges. These can be as basic as breathing or as complex as the desire for a new iPhone. Instant gratification is the desire to satisfy these needs and wants without delay. This is the opposite of what those with mental toughness practice—delayed gratification.

Delayed gratification is the practice of waiting for what you want. Waiting is hard, but it allows you to flex your mental toughness muscle. Constantly indulging in instant gratification often manifests as procrastination; you would rather indulge in a giant slice of chocolate cake than go for a run or surf the Internet instead of finish a course paper.

These choices to pamper yourself through instant gratification can ultimately hamper your ability to reach your long-term goals. Allowing the pleasure principle to take over your decision-making degrades your self-discipline and makes you mentally weak.

In the 1960s, a Stanford professor conducted a well-known psychological test. He gave a series of children a difficult choice: eat one marshmallow now or wait a short time and receive two marshmallows. Predictably, many children chose to eat the single marshmallow immediately. Some children tried to wait but quickly gave in and ate the marshmallow. It was a small percentage of the children that were able to successfully wait and receive the second marshmallow.

The outcome of the experiment is not surprising. What is surprising is what happened to these children when they grew up. The children that were able to wait to receive the second marshmallow grew up to be more successful, were less likely to be obese or have substance abuse issues, had higher SAT scores, and generally had better scores on other measures of life success.

In life, success usually comes down to being able to choose the pain of discipline over the easier choice of rest or distraction. These children, at a very young age, were exhibiting self-discipline. They were able to choose the pain of mental toughness and set themselves up to face the realities of life.

These findings led another group of researchers to wonder whether the ability to delay gratification and wait for the second marshmallow was an innate ability, something the children were born with, or a learned ability. To find the answer they designed a second experiment. In this experiment the children were divided into two groups: one group was exposed to a series of unreliable events and the other group was exposed to only very reliable events.

Unreliable events included situations such as researchers promising to bring the children nicer crayons and a better selection of stickers but never following through on these promises. On the other hand, the children that were exposed to reliable experiences were promised the same crayons and stickers, but the researchers kept the promise and returned with the new items.

Both groups of children were later exposed to the original marshmallow experiment. As you might be able to guess, the group of children that were exposed to unreliable experiences had no reason to expect the researchers to bring a second marshmallow, so they quickly ate the single marshmallow.

On the other hand, the group of children that had only reliable experiences with the researchers was able to wait, on average, four times longer to obtain the second marshmallow. The children that had reliable experiences with the researchers had essentially trained their brains to believe that waiting for gratification was worth it and that they had the capacity to wait. In other words, the child's ability to delay gratification was not an innate ability. The trait can be learned.

If delayed gratification is a learned trait, anyone can practice it or at least improve it to find similar results the children who insisted on waiting for the second marshmallow. By simply setting yourself up to practice the skill of delayed gratification, it can become something that your mind engages in more or less automatically.

Making the choice to forego short-term pleasure in order to gain increased long-term satisfaction and rewards is the very spirit of building the skill of mental toughness. By warding off the short-term temptations, you are able to stay laser-focused on the long-term outcomes. In some cases, this might cause short-term suffering or a certain level of discomfort, but in the end your long-term goals are worth a bit of pain! We already know that short-term discomfort only makes you better and stronger.

Getting into the habit of delaying gratification gives you more control over your life, decisions, and habits. It also helps you to understand the value of hard work and effort. Choosing to delay gratification helps to strengthen your mind and shape your character. It builds self-control, willpower, self-discipline, and the value of patience. It is one habit that can be used to gauge how successful you will become and what you will achieve in life.

Curious about how to practice delayed gratification so you can benefit from the skill?

First, stop thinking about short-term pleasures. It sounds simple, but if you are constantly surrounded by temptation it can be tricky. If this is true for you, you must immediately change your environment to hide, or remove, the temptations. The more difficult it becomes to access temptations, the less likely you will be to indulge in them. Staying focused and on-task when problems arise is in large part a matter of the type of environment you construct for yourself.

This is the reason that health experts often recommend placing healthy food choices in the front of your refrigerator or out on the kitchen counter while hiding or throwing away unhealthy choices. Mentally tough individuals know that reaching long-term goals requires the ability to stay focused and on-task—key traits in delayed gratification.

After you have adjusted your environment to stop thinking about short-term pleasures, you need to focus on not making excuses for your behavior. Quit justifying your actions.

I'm feeling a little hungry. Maybe I'll just eat some of these potato chips before I meet Carol for dinner in 10 minutes.

This is a brand-new episode of my favorite show! I better watch it right now instead of cleaning the kitchen. It might not come on again this evening.

If thoughts like these have crossed your mind, you are trying to justify your actions. This won't help you cultivate mental toughness or learn the habit of delayed gratification. There is never a good excuse for indulging in temptations. You may think that you are indulging to distract you from your problems, but this is only a lie you have created to make yourself feel better. It might feel like you truly lack the physical or mental ability to resist, but in the end, that's also another excuse.

Eating ice cream for dinner because you had a hard day at work or deciding to skip the gym because you feel a little tired are both examples of indulgent behavior disguised as a distraction from problems. If you find yourself frequently making excuses for your behavior of indulging in instant gratification, try changing your internal dialogue to replace the excuse with the real reason and the literal thing you cannot delay.

I'm feeling a little hungry. Maybe I'll just eat some of these potato chips before I meet Carol for dinner in 10 minutes.

Becomes:

I lack willpower and mental toughness and delay eating for 20 minutes.

This is a brand-new episode of my favorite show! I better watch it right now instead of cleaning the kitchen. It might not come on again this evening.

Becomes:

I am lazy and want to procrastinate on everything. I cannot delay watching television.

It's almost a bit startling at how you find yourself characterized, by yourself, when you try to see things from a literal standpoint. Instead of proactively making excuses for yourself, you may be able to delay gratification by proactively vilifying yourself.

Another effective way to delay gratification is to invest your extra time, effort, and energy into future gains. You should be pursuing long-term pleasures and rewards. To do this, consider every action through the lens of what you are likely to gain in the future. Sure, going to the gym tonight is tough, but you will be more fit in the future and possibly increase your lifespan. Choosing to work on your big presentation now, instead of heading out to happy hour with friends, may seem torturous, but you will be more prepared during the event and might even score an advancement or at least kudos from your boss.

Absolutely, some tasks will seem monotonous or boring, but when you zoom out on your timeline you will be reminded that it is all part of the bigger picture and will lead to significant future gains. This reminder, in and of itself, may be enough to motivate you to move forward. You are always weighing your future benefits against your present desires and temptations.

We very rarely get something for nothing in life. This is especially true when considering our long-term goals. You will undoubtedly need to move through quite a bit of short-term pain and discomfort, whether it's putting in lots of long weekend runs or taking on a side hustle, to achieve success. You may even have to make severe sacrifices or go through unimaginable struggles along the way, and it is precisely at these points that you will have to flex your mental toughness muscle the strongest and engage in self-discipline to avoid giving in to instant gratification. You must resist the temptation to succumb to your urges and the pleasure principle.

In order to become mentally tough, you must practice engaging your mental toughness in many small ways, every day. Avoid allowing the pleasure principle to influence your actions, and practice delayed gratification for greater future rewards. No one will be mentally tough on day one; just like any muscle, your mental toughness muscle needs to be used and stretched to grow strong.

The 40% Rule

An easy way to think about building the skill of mental toughness is to borrow from Navy SEALs. Of course, these are elite soldiers that are known for pushing their boundaries—after all, their lives can depend on it. They intimately know that the human body and mind can push far more than we give it credit for. This is known as the 40% rule.

The 40% rule is straightforward. It says that when an individual's mind begins telling them that they are physically or emotionally maxed out, in reality they have only pushed themselves to 40% of their full capacity. In other words, they could endure 60% more if only they believed that they are capable of it. When you think you have reached your limits, you're not even close, and whether you can keep going or not depends on if you believe it. It's quite a belief to feel that you've reached your limits and say to yourself that you're only 40% done. It's an acceptance of pain.

We are usually ready to give up around the time that we begin to feel pain or are barely pressing our boundaries. But that point is actually just the beginning of what we are all capable of, and the key to unlocking more potential is to push through the initial pain and the self-doubt that surfaces along

144

with it. By maintaining a belief in yourself, you show yourself that you can do more, and that evidence builds your confidence and mental toughness.

You might, for example, begin struggling after doing 10 push-ups. You'd start hearing the voice in your head that says you feel too tired, too sore, or too weak to go on. But if you take a pause and gather yourself to do one more, you find that you've already disproven the voice saying that you can't. Then you pause and do another. And then another.

And then another. Suddenly you're at 20. You can take it slowly, but you've just doubled what you thought was possible, just because you kept pushing.

Believing that you can do more will make it true, and this in itself is a skill to build. It enables you to go well beyond the limits that you've constructed for yourself in your own mind. And once you've felt the pain and the urge to give up at 10 push-ups only to push through it and do 20, you know that your mental strength helped you persevere. The next time you're challenged, you'll feel all the more capable and prepared to push past your supposed limits again. This embodies mental toughness in a nutshell— it's really a matter of how much pain you can stomach, and most of us will only bend and never break.

Our minds can be our best friends when we have a strong belief in our capabilities, but they can also be a poisonous enemy if we allow negativity to seize control. It's up to you to empower yourself using the 40% rule rather than throwing in the towel mentally at the first sign of resistance.

Imagine that you decide to run a 5k or even a full marathon despite being out of shape. Inevitably, as you run you'll begin to breathe harder, your legs will feel heavier, and you might question yourself. You could easily give up in that moment and save yourself from extra pain and soreness. But if circumstances were different and you were running away from danger out of self-preservation, you could undoubtedly continue on well beyond that first inclination to give in. Barring massive injuries, you'd finish if you believed the pain was part of the process. It's all a matter of whether you believe you can or not.

The reality is, most of us have no clue about our true physical and mental limitations. Our lives are so much safer and more comfortable than those of our ancestors, and that has some undesirable consequences when it comes to mental toughness. We don't test ourselves and we don't know what we're capable of. Now it is mostly the people who seek out intense challenges that subsequently learn discipline and mental strength, while the rest go about their comfortable lives without any idea of their full capabilities.

In case you're skeptical as to the merits of the 40% rule, there is some scientific evidence in support of it that might help convince you. Numerous studies over the years have found that the placebo effect— the tangible change in performance caused merely by a belief that something you've done will impact performance—has a significant impact, especially in athletics. The legitimacy of the placebo effect suggests that your mental strength and toughness plays a big role in physical abilities. In other words, if you believe it, it will *be*.

There is a scientific consensus that the placebo effect is not a deception, fluke, experimental bias, or statistical anomaly. Rather, it is a self-fulfilling prophecy in which the human brain anticipates an outcome and then produces that outcome of its own accord. In fact, the placebo effect closely follows the types of patterns you would expect to see if the brain was really producing its own desired results. Researchers have illustrated this phenomenon by showing that placebos follow the same dose-response curves as real medicines. Two pills give more relief than one, a larger pill has a stronger effect than a smaller one, and so on.

When you consider the placebo effect, it quickly becomes clear how powerful our minds are. Countless studies have supported the conclusion that the placebo effect is a result of chemical changes in the form of endorphin production. Just believing that you can give 60% more effort makes it possible.

For any goals that you have, struggles with discipline can probably be overcome by changing your expectations. Whenever you find yourself making excuses or lacking mental toughness, consider the 40% rule and the placebo effect and ask if your excuses are legitimate. Expecting yourself to be capable, successful, and disciplined will make it all the more likely that you actually are.

Navy SEALs employ another valuable technique that is centered around battling the negative physical effects of stress and anxiety. When you can control your arousal and emotional state, you can control how you react far better. This also works to help with emotional reasoning as it reverses emotion's effects on the body.

As a result of hundreds of thousands of years of evolution, we have developed knee-jerk reactions and neurochemical responses to stimulation that are often highly undesirable when it comes to performing optimally. The fight-or-flight response is one of these, which puts you into a state of massive physiological arousal and makes your mind go blank and necessarily lose all discipline and willpower in the interest of survival. These responses indeed contributed to increased chances of survival, but unfortunately, they don't have much of a place in modern society.

Being able to relax and focus in order to avoid distractions from natural stress responses is essential for mental toughness. We secrete hormones in large doses when we are under high stress or experiencing a good deal of fear, and controlling those secretions in the moment is next to impossible for us.

For Navy SEALs, however, succumbing to undesirable responses will mean the difference between life and death. As you might expect, they have some techniques that help them maintain clear mental states even in the most dangerous and stressful environments. One of those techniques that anybody can easily use is what's known as box breathing. This means that when SEALs recognize that they are feeling overwhelmed, they regain control by focusing on their breath—breathing in for four seconds, holding for four seconds, and then out for four seconds, and repeating until you can feel your heart rate slow down and normalize. Its beauty is in its simplicity.

A stressed-out mind is a mentally weak and emotional mind, so it is crucial for you to be able to remain calm if you want to perform to your full potential. Box breathing is simple to implement, and if it works for Navy SEALs, it can certainly work for us. The technique itself is easy, but the real key is to be able to recognize when your arousal might spiral out of control and sabotage your mental toughness.

Whenever you feel your heart beginning to race or your palms beginning to sweat, try focusing on your breath to reign in your undesirable reactions. If you can use box breathing at the first hint of physical arousal or stress, you will fare well because you will be able to control it. It's easier to stop it rather than manage it.

Meditation practices also often involve focusing on the breath and have a similar effect of reducing fight-or-flight instincts. However you go about it, controlling arousal can make a world of difference. Maybe it's the next time you're anxiously anticipating speaking in front of an audience or perhaps taking an intense and important exam. Whatever it is that causes you stress, you'll be more adept to handle it with a clear mental state.

Takeaways:

• Categorizing mental toughness as a skill rather than a trait has value because skills can be learned but also need time and hard work. Mental toughness does not arise out of nowhere in people. What are some ways we can work to increase our mental toughness skillset?

- It's really about putting yourself in situations where you must exercise your self-discipline and mental toughness on a daily, continual basis. There are daily actions you can practice, such as taking a cold shower or eating raw garlic cloves—but the main idea is to choose to put yourself into an uncomfortable position often to build up your tolerance levels.

- Mental toughness can also be said to be the epitome of delaying gratification. Instant gratification is when you choose your present self over your future self— we know how poorly that decision will turn out. You can practice delaying gratification by recognizing the difference between your present self and future self and also by replacing your excuses for instant gratification (I was hungry) for the unfiltered truth (I couldn't resist eating; I have no willpower).

- Unsurprisingly, Navy SEALs can teach us quite a bit about mental toughness.

Their very lives depend on their ability to manipulate their psyches into persevering states. Two big lessons are the 40% rule, which states that when we think we are done, we are actually only at 40% of our capacity, and the importance of controlling our arousal and emotional states through box breathing.

Chapter 6. Build the Daily Habit

Ancient Chinese philosopher Sun-Tzu said that every battle is won or lost before it is ever fought. In order to establish unshakeable mental toughness, there are habits and mindsets that you can collect and build on every day. If you are scrambling to shore up your mental defenses when an obstacle is staring you in the face, you've already lost. Prepare these habits before you need them in battle and you will be ready to come out on top.

Sammy had never been much of an athlete, but as middle age started to creep up on him he realized he was slowly but steadily gaining weight. His doctor recommended he take up some light exercise and examine his diet. Figuring he could use a little help, he joined a local jogging group.

He started out with some of the beginner runs, short and slow, a few mornings a week. But Sammy quickly realized that on the mornings he accomplished a run first thing, he felt more in control and ready to tackle anything else the day could bring.

The grit that he was building by consistently showing up and pushing himself athletically was transferring over into other areas of his life. Sammy was tapping into a commonly known trick among athletes—diligence and commitment to athletics builds reserves of mental stamina and toughness that can be deployed in all areas of life.

The feelings of power that Sammy was growing during his workouts began to transfer over to his work life, and his admin assistant began to remark on how different he was behaving in the weekly board meetings. Sammy began participating in more of the jogging group's events and even signed up for a 10k. The more involved he became in the jogging group, the more in control and confident he felt.

Ultimately, not only did Sammy lose the weight that was his original goal, but he also revamped his self-confidence and increased his mental toughness by consistently pushing himself physically and discovering new boundaries far outside of his old comfort zone. Sammy had developed his mental toughness muscle through consistent use in his workouts. What started out as a simple slow jog a few mornings a week morphed into a more serious commitment with much more serious mental toughness requirements.

Visualization

Visualization is another habit that can be used to build mental toughness. Mental rehearsal, or visualization, is a technique that athletes, musicians, doctors, soldiers, and even astronauts use to prepare for any possibility and perform at their best. To engage in mental rehearsal you envision an event or scenario that is making you nervous or that you need to be prepared for. Start at the very beginning and imagine each step of the process or event, including possible hiccups and your reaction to them.

For example, an athlete can use mental rehearsal to visualize scoring goals or imagining the most effective way to block an opponent's advances. A doctor might use mental rehearsal to prepare for a unique surgery by envisioning each step of the procedure and possible complications. You may not be an athlete or a doctor, but you can apply the techniques of mental rehearsal to almost anything you do in your daily life. By mentally rehearsing challenges you expect to face or areas of your life that could be more efficient, you are forcing yourself to think through overcoming or improving these situations.

We worry about things because we feel we are not fully prepared to face them. At its base, mental rehearsal allows you to convince yourself that you are prepared. It lets you identify the source of your worries, create alternative plans in case of unexpected events, and walk through the event a few times until you feel prepared. After mentally rehearsing an upcoming situation or event, your worries will seem to melt away.

To mentally rehearse an event, begin by imagining yourself walking into a movie theater. You are on the big screen, performing whatever actions you are worried about. Start at the very beginning. If you are worried about an upcoming presentation, start your mental rehearsal before the presentation. What will you do the day before to create the materials? How will you arrange the room? When you get to a point that has the potential to go wrong, try to imagine all the possibilities and what you will do in each circumstance. Go through this step for every possible situation, from the tiniest mistake to an absolute worst-case scenario.

Make sure to visualize every single detail. If you will be wearing a suit, imagine yourself wearing the suit in your mental rehearsal. Will you be sitting or standing? Incorporate that into your visualization. Mentally rehearse until you see the situation realistically.

By going through these steps, you are identifying and converting the things you are worried about into a more approachable form. You're creating a to-do list of things that you have control over and can plan for. Mentally rehearsing forces you to be more prepared for an event and also allows you to release the anxiety that surrounds it.

Althea was concerned about an upcoming swim meet. To decrease her anxiety, she could engage in mental rehearsal. The beginning of her mental rehearsal might look something like this:

"I'll arrive at the meet 30 minutes early, parking as close to the door as possible. Walking into the locker room, I'll get out my

suit, cap, and goggles. After changing, I will walk out and begin my warm-up. For a warm-up I will dive in and swim 400 meters freestyle. It's possible that there may be too many other swimmers in the warm-up lanes.

If this happens, I will do my stretching before I do my warm-up swimming instead of afterward. After completing my warm-up swimming and stretching, I'll grab my towel and rehydrate. If there is nowhere to sit, I'll head back into the locker room. I know that my race is one of the first, so I'll go through some muscle relaxation and then walk to the starting block.

Standing on the starting block, I will probably feel nervous, but I will focus on the water and executing my dive perfectly. Once in the water, I will specifically concentrate on my stroke—arm movements are that area that my coach said I needed to improve to place in this race. For each stroke I will make sure that I reach my arms up as far as possible and bring them down swiftly beside my ear.

My pace should follow my breathing. 'Stroke, stroke, breath, stroke, stroke, breath.'"

By engaging in this mental rehearsal and seeing it through to the end of her race, Althea can think through possible complications such as not having a free warm-up swim lane and feeling nervous on the starting block. This will enable her to release some of the worry that she has and feel more in control of the events.

Visualization creates the overall feeling that you'll be fine, that you can handle what might come your way, and that ultimately you'll find success. As we know, belief is a large component of mental toughness.

Emulate Athletes

Just like Sammy in our opening example, athletes have long known that building mental toughness and endurance through physical feats primes mental toughness for other areas in our lives.

There are many things that we can learn and apply to our own lives from athletes and other similar people who perform under high pressure on a daily basis. Their entire jobs are to perform accurately and consistently under very high pressure with extremely high stakes. Athletes know that the grit that it takes to apply physical discipline to your life begets mental toughness. If you do challenging physical things on a daily, weekly, or monthly basis you will be able to think, "I accomplished that, so I can definitely accomplish the task in front of me right now."

Many people use mental toughness to increase their physical fitness, but it can also work the opposite way. Roman Legionnaires would routinely be required to carry around approximately 28 pounds of weapons, armor, and equipment. They were forced to carry this weight into battle and on marches of up to 35 miles per day. Modern-day airborne infantrymen in Afghanistan may carry up to 127 pounds depending on the mission and travel for hundreds of miles.

Although we aren't required to carry this amount of gear in our everyday lives, it doesn't mean that we can't apply these warrior principles to ourselves. We can still choose to build up our bodies through the habit of physical discipline and therefore build our mental toughness. Choosing to run a marathon or compete in a Tough Mudder are options, but you don't have to be that extreme to gain the benefits of this habit. Simply showing up consistently and pushing yourself further, faster, or harder than you did the day before will also work to build this habit and grow your mental toughness.

Set Performance Cues

Another habit that is employed by mentally tough individuals is the decision to set performance cues.

According to the Association of Applied Sports Psychology, a performance cue statement is a short statement said to yourself to refocus your concentration.

These cues help you to focus regardless of the challenging environment, difficult situation, or negative obtrusive thoughts that you might find swirling through your brain.

They help to limit the impact these negative aspects may have on your performance. The use of self-talk, motivational phrases, and even Internet memes is not new. The goal is to find a word or phrase that connects personally to you. Link this word or phrase to a highly memorable moment such as driving the ball far down range to sink a hole in one or the handshake at the end of an important sales meeting when you bagged the client. Then use this word or phrase in similar situations to focus yourself.

In 1997, a group of researchers wanted to determine if assigning specific cue words to athletes to use during their event would allow them to more efficiently execute their race and consequently run more quickly. The researchers took a group of elite national-level track sprinters and assembled them in Australia. On average, these athletes could run the 100-meter in 10 seconds. They were given three cue words, one for each portion of their race. The cue words were designed to sum up the phase of the race and to be as short as possible to avoid misinterpretation.

For the first 30 meters of the race, the athletes' cue word was "push." This emphasized the importance of acceleration during this portion of the run. For the second 30 meters, the cue word was "heel" because the athletes were hitting their peak speed. And for the final 40 meters of the race, athletes were asked to use the cue word "claw." This was the endurance section of the race and the cue word "claw" was meant to inspire them to hang on and keep going until the finish line.

Amazingly, of the 12 runners that were studied, all but one improved significantly with the use of the cue words. The one runner that did not have a significant improvement ran identical times with and without the cues. The average drop in time was 0.26 seconds, which is astronomical for the distance being run. This 0.26-second improvement represents over a 2% increase in speed. This is particularly exciting when you remember that all it took to see such an increase in speed was the recitation of some cue words.

On top of the increase in speed, the runners also performed more consistently. The variance in finish time was only 0.15 seconds in comparison to the control group, which had a variance of 0.38 seconds. When asked why they believed the cue words improved their performance so drastically, the runners noted that the cue words kept their minds from wandering and they helped keep them focused on executing their technique.

Keeping 100% focused is challenging, especially in high-pressure situations. Using the cue words is a powerful tool because they can keep you from feeling overwhelmed. The cues also provide something to focus on that you have control over. Your brain can only truly focus on one thing at a time, and cue words ensure that your focus remains on your performance. They also serve as an anchor to keep your thoughts from wandering during a physical or mental challenge.

Because the cue words selected for the sprinters were technical, they forced the athletes to hone in on their technique at critical points in the race. Overall, the runners found that their form and stride didn't break down as fast as normal. The right cue words can increase our motivation and also keep us laser-focused on what we need to be doing at each moment.

To employ cue words in your everyday life and cultivate this habit of mental toughness, simply hone in on a word or phrase that has meaning to you. It can be related to performance, such as "claw," "push," and "heel" were in the example experiment, or simply remind you of a time that you were extremely successful. Then build the habit of mentally reciting this word in situations where you need to focus or shut out distractions. As simple as that, you have

168

built a mental toughness habit into your life and you can reap the benefits of increased focus and greater efficiency.

Accept Uncertainty

The last powerful habit to embrace to build mental toughness is to accept uncertainty. This is the act of letting go and relinquishing your expectations over how your life should unfold.

There's no possible way for us to control everything in our world. Trying to do so is usually a surefire recipe for chaos, inefficiency, and massive disappointment. You should take this as *good* news, at least a little, since it removes a great amount of expectation off your shoulders and makes it easier for you to envision surviving.

Because of it, we therefore have to allow the reality that we'll always have a certain degree of uncertainty in our lives. We don't know where we'll be five years from now, who will come into or exit from our lives, how successful we'll be, or how long we'll live. But not knowing the outcome shouldn't be the source of additional pressure or nervousness. Simply accepting a lack of control is freeing and builds your mental toughness because suddenly you're not anchored by unrealistic expectations.

Cognitive therapist Dr. Robert Leahy explains why dread over the uncertain can be such a drain for those susceptible to such fears. "People worry because they think something bad will happen or could happen, so they activate a hyper-vigilant strategy of worry and think that 'If I worry I can prevent this bad thing from happening or catch it early.'"

We believe that if anything unexpected happens to come up in the course of work, then it's going to end badly. Uncertainty is an assumed precursor to a negative event. Uncertainty equals disaster. Therefore, we hold predictability as the highest standard and volatile unpredictability as the lowest.

Of course, it's important to be as smart and thoughtful as possible about potential hazards that could arise in any activity, as long as it's done from a pragmatic standpoint.

A healthier mindset doesn't just leave room for uncertainty—it *accepts* it. Anything else and you're just waiting for something that has never been possible and is never going to show itself to you. You must come to terms with a low degree of background discomfort in your life; if it suddenly vanishes completely, it's a good sign that you're not doing anything worthwhile and have little reason to utilize mental toughness.

You have no choice but to live with this uncertainty—so acceptance of it is just a step above that. Understand the possible results of the uncertainty: you might not be in the same place next week. But right now, you're not in the same place you were five years ago. You weren't able to see the future back then any more than you are now, and you're still here. What's different about this situation?

Accept the reality, digest it, and allow that there's no immediate resolution—then continue doing what you need to do.

I know what you're saying: "If we accept uncertainty and merrily embrace it, then what happens when we really *do* get a terrible outcome? Won't this cause us to underestimate how awful the uncertain thing really is? What if acceptance of whatever's out there causes us to disregard warning signs or cautions and the whole thing becomes a catastrophe because we 'accepted uncertainty'? And then won't we be haunted by remorse for the rest of our lives because we didn't do enough?"

That's understandable. But I didn't say to *ignore* the possibility of uncertain, adverse events. Accepting uncertainty isn't the same thing as dismissing it as irrelevant. Getting absolute certainty is impossible—it will never happen. You'll just continue to worry about it and will never feel settled. And some things will always be outside of your control, no matter how much you worry about them.

Think about this: how much uncertainty do you already allow in your life as a regular occurrence? Every time you get in a vehicle you're subjecting yourself to the unknown. Any time you change cities, change jobs, or take a vacation, there's a number of risks that you're taking. But they're not standing in the way of your work or your leisure. Why are they any different? We take these for granted and ignore the fact that we never associate them with negative outcomes.

Most worriers will admit that all those everyday risks are things they accept because giving them too much credence will keep them from living a normal life. Absolutely true. So what makes your worries about *non*-daily events—the work presentation, the marriage proposal, the final exam—any harder to handle? Recall that we hate uncertainty because we see a very clear cause-and-effect relationship. If you were to make a list of daily uncertainties you face and record the consequences, you'll slowly be able to destroy that relationship.

173

If you can bring the attitude you have toward everyday, unremarkable "worries" to these more extraordinary situations, you might find a whole lot of relief and progress happening. Trudging through these worries and changing your perspective on them is how you survive them.

If the notion of accepting uncertainty reminds you of Buddhism's insistence on the impermanence of life, you'd be right to make that connection. They both present different ways of perceiving the world to become more resilient and difficult to knock down. When you can accept that the world has no obligation to go your way, you've instantly become more adaptable and mentally tough.

Takeaways:

• Battles are usually won far before they actually begin. This means we should build our foundation of mental toughness far before we need it. If we are grasping for it in the heat of the moment, it's probably too late. We're going to lose. Ideally, we engage in a few habits to make mental toughness an unconscious response.

- Visualization is a helpful habit. Otherwise known as mental rehearsal, it is when you view yourself going through that what you fear most. View yourself dealing with it in incredible detail, down to every last pen stroke. This allows you to understand what you'll need to deal with and prepare yourself for the likelihood of obstacles. Overall, you become more prepared and confident in your abilities to adapt.

- Get into the habit of emulating athletes in the sense of pursuing physical excellence. For most, mental toughness begets physical toughness. It can also work the other way around—building the habit of physical toughness can give your psyche plenty of evidence to remain confident and tough. Similarly, use performance cues to call attention to the fact that you're not "in the zone."

- Learn to accept uncertainty on a daily basis. We struggle to do this because we tend to associate uncertainty with negative outcomes. But letting go of expectations of certainty and control will instantly make you more adaptable and understanding of hardship.

Chapter 7. Pitfalls to Avoid

Austin had always been pretty confident about his writing ability. He received frequent praise in high school, college, and during his first few positions after graduation. It wasn't until he started working for a large newspaper that he began receiving constructive criticism and other unsolicited advice from his more experienced coworkers.

Austin generally shrugged off the advice because he felt confident in his ability and experience. After all, no one had ever criticized him before, so he thought he was still correct about everything.

One day, about four months after starting at the newspaper, he was called into his editor's office. In no uncertain terms he was told exactly what aspects of his writing he should focus on to improve. At first, Austin shrugged off this direction as well, but after some reflection time he decided to take his editor's advice to heart and try to improve specific aspects of his work. By applying the advice that was given to him by his editor and coworkers, he was ultimately able to improve his craft and continue to grow toward his career goals.

We all make mistakes while striving to achieve mental toughness and reach our long-term goals. Just like Austin, we may have trouble taking constructive criticism to heart, or we may struggle with accepting things we cannot change or wrestle with letting go of things that we cannot control. But whatever our mistakes, there are methods to overcome them and continue to learn and grow. Identifying these mistakes is half the battle. The remainder of this chapter will list some of the most common mistakes in achieving resilience and give instructions for conquering them.

Wanting Control

A common mistake made by individuals trying to increase their mental toughness is to spend too much time focusing on things they cannot control. In some respects, this is similar to the concept of accepting uncertainty from the previous chapter. Once you let go of the compulsion for control, you realize that you are equipped to handle a wide variety of situations.

The key to toughness is to focus specifically on the things you can control and deliberately ignore the rest.

There are many things in your life that are out of your control: other people's opinions of you, whether a new business will succeed or fail, and your supervisor's treatment of you. However, you can control your own actions, how you speak to and interact with others, how much effort you put into a new business, and how you behave at work. No matter how much you focus on things that are out of your control, you can't change them. It's a waste of time and effort to try, and it saps your mental toughness because you're putting in work for no certain reward.

We can control our input into a situation, but not the outcome. It is up to us to ensure that we are putting our greatest effort into each situation for the best possible outcome. But focusing on too many additional things, especially those that are out of your control, only succeeds in reducing your willpower and distracting you from areas in which your effort can have an effect.

You cannot control how an important conference call goes, but it is completely in your control to be as prepared and ready to positively represent your product as possible. Similarly, you cannot force your coworkers to like you, but you can give 100% at work and consistently treat them with respect and courtesy. When you focus on yourself and let go of the rest, you'll feel empowered and free. Identify areas in which you have control and you will get the most impact for your effort.

Mindset Differences

There are some very specific habits of mind that illuminate the difference in thinking between mentally tough and mentally weak individuals. In the following section, we will look at specific mistakes that people make that undermine their mental toughness.

Hard work matters. Mentally tough individuals know that hard work is the only way to achieve their goals. It is only through this hard work, self-discipline, and grit that they can move toward success and the life that they want to lead. There is a direct correlation, and the belief in hard work propels people into action.

Mentally weak individuals often feel as if the world owes them something. They don't believe that they need to work or exercise self-control to get what they want. They feel that success is something they should be handed simply because they exist. You may have encountered this type of mentally weak individual at work. Hallmarks of this thought process include a general disregard of rules, because rules "don't apply to them," and an expectation of recognition or promotion for every project they complete.

Know where your values come from. Mentally tough people know where their values come from. This means they don't need external praise or recognition to reinforce their self-confidence. They already know that they are good at their jobs, are dedicated to their family, or are excellent friends, and they don't need someone to tell them this to believe it. They know who they are, what they care about, and how they would like to represent themselves to the world.

On the other hand, mentally weak people crave this recognition and without it they feel inadequate or overlooked. Mentally weak people undervalue their worth and lack self-confidence. Hallmarks of this thought process include constantly fishing for compliments or kudos.

Self-reflection. Time for self-reflection is vital to mentally strong people. Determining the motivation behind their actions and desires is an important habit of mind that they actively cultivate. Knowing what motivates you and what discourages you allows you to seek more good and avoid the bad. Self-reflection also allows mentally tough individuals to think about and learn from mistakes and other past experiences.

Mentally weak individuals do not take the time to be self-reflective. These people are self-indulgent and do what they want, when they want, without regard for their motivations or other people's feelings. They are driven by their emotions and cannot keep their compulsions in check. They simply don't know why they are acting the way they do. To identify these weak individuals, look for hasty, poorly considered decisions and inconsistent actions.

Embrace alone time. Mentally tough people are comfortable with themselves. They understand their actions, feel their emotions, and relish time by themselves. These mentally tough individuals enjoy the company of others, but they don't feel the need to constantly surround themselves with friends or acquaintances. However, those without this level of self-confidence and ease in their own body feel anxious when they aren't surrounded by others to compliment or reassure them about their own self-worth. These mentally weak people always need company and feel like a failure if they are sitting at home alone on a Friday night.

Being tired isn't an excuse. Mentally tough people don't give in when they are tired. They understand that 95% of the time they still have energy left, and this "tiredness" is just a feeling they can shrug off. Everyone gets tired, so how can that ever be a justification?

Weak individuals jump off the treadmill as soon as they feel tired, hit the snooze button three or four times before getting out of bed, or procrastinate an important project because they would rather spend some time resting in front of the TV. To exercise your mental toughness, don't give in! You still have some gas in your tank; just push through this tired feeling and keep striving to achieve your goals. Of course, this encompasses elements of the 40% rule and delaying gratification.

Pain can be positive. Don't be afraid of pain for the greater good. Cold showers, raw garlic, and refusing to hit the snooze are painful in the moment but they ultimately build a stronger, more disciplined mind. Embrace discomfort and actively seek out situations where you must display willpower.

Mentally weak individuals shy away from pain, even though it will help them achieve their long-term goals. Getting through pain is an essential part of achieving success in life, and mentally tough individuals know this and refuse to view short-term pain as anything other than an obstacle to overcome on their path to success.

Deal with the truth. Be realistic about your strengths and weaknesses. We all have areas to improve, and mentally tough people know that they are awesome in tons of ways, but they are also realistic about areas where they need a little more work. It's in accepting our weaknesses that we can approach and improve them.

Our parents always told us that we could be anything and that we were the most incredible human to ever walk the Earth. For mentally weak people, this still rings true. They often have trouble identifying their areas of weakness or being honest about mistakes they have made. When confronted with their weaknesses or mistakes, mentally weak people run or refuse to acknowledge them.

Only those who are mentally tough can take these criticisms and incorporate the advice to make themselves stronger and more resilient. The next time your boss suggests areas in which you could improve, take these suggestions to heart. You're not perfect, regardless of what your parents said, and we all have skills that could use a little more work.

Don't be too sensitive. Don't let other people's opinions or problems impact your life. Mentally tough people know that they don't need to alter their day or change their feelings based on someone else's problems, feelings, to-do list, or preferences. If your coworker yells at you because he is having a bad day or if your girlfriend stomps out of the apartment because she had a fight with her mom, you can't internalize these incidents and let them impact your plans or goals for the day.

Stop letting other people have an impact on your destiny. Only the mentally weak let other people's problems derail their day; it's a waste of time and energy. Of course, you will need to remain empathetic, but you also need to realize that you are not responsible for carrying the burdens of others.

Being average is not okay. Mentally tough people know not to stop pushing and working at something when they become adequate. Being average is never enough for someone with grit and determination. Those with mental strength want to be the best version of themselves that they can be and won't stop until they achieve this goal.

Being a mediocre student or average wife should never be enough. Mentally tough people won't settle for being in the middle of the pack. Always strive to run a slightly faster race, create a slightly better chicken Parmesan, or close on slightly more homes than you did the previous month. Inching forward over time and becoming better at your hobby, job, or relationship ensures that you never fall into the trap of mediocrity.

It's not enough to be okay at something—you need to be performing at your peak. This by definition requires mental toughness—but the act of pursuing will grant you mental toughness.

Kaizen

Going from zero to insane mental toughness is unrealistic. It's a mistake that stems from expectations that are too high. When you inevitably fall short of your imagined progress, it's likely that you'll become discouraged and depressed. Instead, focusing on small, continuous improvement is the true path to gaining mental toughness.

You won't be mentally tough tomorrow, but over time you will reach your desired level of grit and self-discipline. This rings true for every aspect of life you want to improve, but it is doubly important in mental toughness because it involves a delicate mental state.

Depression-era American business managers developed a method of improvement designed to help the United States win World War II. It was based on

189

the idea of continuous improvement in a thousand small ways. These business managers told American companies to focus on small improvements throughout their company. A manual created by the U.S. government advised factory supervisors to "look for hundreds of small things you can improve. Don't try to plan a whole new departmental layout—or go after a big installation of new equipment. There isn't time for these major items. Look for improvements on existing jobs with your present equipment."

After America defeated Japan and Germany in World War II using weapons and other products created in these factories operating under the small, continuous improvement philosophy, they passed the idea on to the Japanese to assist in the rebuilding efforts. The idea of small, continuous improvement caught on immediately in Japan and was named *Kaizen*.

While this idea of Kaizen was originally created with business improvement in mind, it is just as applicable to our personal lives. Making small, incremental improvements on a daily basis may not seem like much initially, but they will gradually lead to the change you want to see. Focus on a 1% daily improvement. It originally might not seem like much, but that 1% compounds until you begin to notice improvements in your life. Choose to eat that daily raw clove of garlic, ignore the desire to skip the gym because of a hard day at work, or refuse to hit the snooze! Making the small daily choices, that 1% improvement that distinguishes today from yesterday, sets you on the path to improved mental toughness and self-discipline. These tiny changes become habit and slowly but surely snowball into noticeable improvements.

The Kaizen method of improvement goes beyond the constant ups and downs of traditional approaches. It forces you to break down goals into small, discrete steps and tackle each step one at a time. Kaizen encourages you to take action and your successes eventually snowball into bigger and bigger actions until you reach your desired goal. Don't seek drastic changes; just seek to do what you can with what you have and go from there.

There is no magic bullet to fix all your problems or enable you to instantly become mentally tough; however, through small, consistent improvement, you can get there. Stop wasting your time searching for the miracle cure or the single habit to change everything. Instead, focus on the task at hand. Do what you need to do and get to work. Do 1% better than the day before and increase your skill gradually. Take it slow and steady. There is a reason that Aesop told us that the tortoise beat the hare— slow and steady wins the race. Mental toughness may not be a flipped switch away, but it is always visible on the horizon.

Takeaways:

- We all make mistakes on a daily basis, and gaining mental toughness is no different. We routinely fall prey to these pitfalls without realizing how detrimental they can be.

- Do you always want control, even the illusion of it? This drains your mental toughness because it makes you fragile in the face of a loss of control—which is always imminent.

- Do you have the expectation of massive change in a short amount of time? This drains your mental toughness because you'll always fall short of this high expectation. Instead, seek to implement a Japanese concept known as *Kaizen*, which is seeking continual, small improvements.

- Here are some traits that differ between individuals with and without mental toughness: recognizing the importance of hard work, knowing your self-values, engaging in self-reflection, seeking alone time, not using fatigue as an excuse, seeing pain as positivity, seeing yourself objectively, being less sensitive, and not settling for mediocrity.

Summary Guide

Chapter 1. The Case of Mental Toughness

- Mental toughness is more than a trait; it's a way of looking at life. Life is tough, so you better get a helmet. Point being, adversity and failure aren't things to plan around—that is impossible. What we should be doing is planning for them and thinking to the next step of how we will react and get back up. That is mental toughness at its core.

- Surprisingly, mental toughness has biological components to it. This manifests mostly in two ways. First, there is an interplay with stressed and rest states, mediated by how strong our amine response is. The stronger the amine response, the less we stress and grow anxious. Second, the concept of ego depletion applies handily to mental toughness. Generally this means that our willpower and discipline wears down with mental fatigue, and it applies to toughness as well. Thankfully, this is something you can plan around if you are aware of it.

- What kind of mantra should you repeat to yourself regarding toughness? It involves adversity, failure, and persistence. Adversity is good, failure is inevitable, and persistence is the secret sauce.

Chapter 2. Facing Failure and Fear

- Can you plan your life to avoid fear and failure? Yes, but that would lead to a life of emptiness. To achieve any measure of happiness and success in life, elements of fear and failure will always be present. Not everything will always go your way. So instead of planning to avoid failure, plan for what happens when you inevitably sail into an iceberg. You may be able to steer clear of the first one, but the second or third will get you eventually.

- Buddhist philosophy is a helpful lens to look at failure through. What is failure to Buddhists? Unpleasant, but impermanent and necessary. Life goes through ebbs and flows, and the only constant is change. Accepting this will help negative moments pass more easily, as will accepting that perfection is impossible. Moreover, our suffering shows us a path to greater fulfillment and happiness. Buddhism is about understanding that your life is like a wave that gives and takes equally.

- Fear and failure are your ultimate teachers. When you fail, typical responses include blaming yourself or denial. These are instinctual because failure is an emotional event, and our lizard brains rush to protect ourselves. But failure is best when you can look at it and give it equal time as your successes. This allows you to understand and deconstruct how to never fail in that context again. Your very worst-case scenario is not failing; it is being able to learn from it.

- *Amor fati* literally means to love fate. Does that mean you should love whatever obstacles or failures you come across? Of course, not. But you can love the infinite possibilities and futures you now have access to. Acceptance, similarly to Buddhism, is important, because to struggle with or deny failure is to cause oneself unnecessary pain.

Chapter 3. Mind Over Heart

- Ultimately, we are all slaves to our emotions. This is an undeniable fact. But at least we can try to battle our lesser instincts and think with logic and reason.
- First, it is important to note that this does not mean suppressing your emotions. In fact, expressing them has been shown to have huge psychological benefits. The more specific and granular you can be with your emotions, the bigger the benefits. It's just a matter of moderation between remaining in control and *feeling*.

- Thinking long-term is a powerful means of remaining calm and rational. When something goes wrong, it may feel like the end of the world, but then what happens when you zoom out? On a long enough timeline, nothing is really very serious. The problem is, we all live in the present moment, but if we were to adjust our expectations and think long-term, we'd understand that we rarely have anything to truly worry about.
- Sometimes when we're emotional, we forget there is going to be a future. Remind yourself by thinking in terms of 10-10-10 and looking toward the rest of your life.
- Finally, a way to build mental toughness and rein in your emotions is to use the ABC loop. ABC stands for Antecedent, Behavior, and Consequence, and they all work together to either reinforce or punish behaviors such as emotional reactions.

Chapter 4. Distorted Realities

- What is a cognitive distortion? It is a pattern of thinking that is unrepresentative of reality. This is significant because most cognitive distortions are disempowering and cause you to doubt yourself, lose confidence, and lose mental toughness. How can you be mentally tough if the world seems to be pitted against you? You're just starting from a place where you can't win.
- Cognitive distortions are often automatic thought patterns that arise from our own insecurities and fears. They aren't totally unfounded, but they depart wildly from reality. They are characterized by jumping to conclusions based on assumptions and incomplete information, as well as overreactions.
- A few of the most well-known and dangerous cognitive distortions are all-or-nothing thinking, personalizing, overgeneralizing, catastrophizing, magnifying and minimizing, and jumping to conclusions. An especially notable cognitive distortion that robs us of resilience is emotional reasoning. This

is when reality is defined by the emotions we feel at that very moment.

Chapter 5. Build the Skill

- Categorizing mental toughness as a skill rather than a trait has value because skills can be learned but also need time and hard work. Mental toughness does not arise out of nowhere in people. What are some ways we can work to increase our mental toughness skillset?
- It's really about putting yourself in situations where you must exercise your self-discipline and mental toughness on a daily, continual basis. There are daily actions you can practice, such as taking a cold shower or eating raw garlic cloves—but the main idea is to choose to put yourself into an uncomfortable position often to build up your tolerance levels.
- Mental toughness can also be said to be the epitome of delaying gratification. Instant gratification is when you choose your present self over your future self— we know how poorly that decision will

turn out. You can practice delaying gratification by recognizing the difference between your present self and future self and also by replacing your excuses for instant gratification (I was hungry) for the unfiltered truth (I couldn't resist eating; I have no willpower).

- Unsurprisingly, Navy SEALs can teach us quite a bit about mental toughness. Their very lives depend on their ability to manipulate their psyches into persevering states. Two big lessons are the 40% rule, which states that when we think we are done, we are actually only at 40% of our capacity, and the importance of controlling our arousal and emotional states through box breathing.

Chapter 6. Build the Daily Habit

- Battles are usually won far before they actually begin. This means we should build our foundation of mental toughness far before we need it. If we are grasping for it in the heat of the moment, it's probably too late. We're going to lose. Ideally, we engage in a few habits to make mental toughness an unconscious response.

- Visualization is a helpful habit. Otherwise known as mental rehearsal, it is when you view yourself going through that what you fear most. View yourself dealing with it in incredible detail, down to every last pen stroke. This allows you to understand what you'll need to deal with and prepare yourself for the likelihood of obstacles. Overall, you become more prepared and confident in your abilities to adapt.

- Get into the habit of emulating athletes in the sense of pursuing physical excellence. For most, mental toughness begets physical toughness. It can also work the other way around—building the habit of physical toughness can give your psyche plenty of evidence to remain confident and tough. Similarly, use performance cues to call attention to the fact that you're not "in the zone."

- Learn to accept uncertainty on a daily basis. We struggle to do this because we tend to associate uncertainty with negative outcomes. But letting go of expectations of certainty and control will instantly make you more adaptable and understanding of hardship.

Chapter 7. Pitfalls to Avoid

- We all make mistakes on a daily basis, and gaining mental toughness is no different. We routinely fall prey to these pitfalls without realizing how detrimental they can be.
- Do you always want control, even the illusion of it? This drains your mental toughness because it makes you fragile in the face of a loss of control—which is always imminent.
- Do you have the expectation of massive change in a short amount of time? This drains your mental toughness because you'll always fall short of this high expectation. Instead, seek to implement a Japanese concept known as *Kaizen*, which is seeking continual, small improvements.

- Here are some traits that differ between individuals with and without mental toughness: recognizing the importance of hard work, knowing your self-values, engaging in self-reflection, seeking alone time, not using fatigue as an excuse, seeing pain as positivity, seeing yourself objectively, being less sensitive, and not settling for mediocrity.

Made in the USA
Las Vegas, NV
26 April 2021